Slurp, Slurp

Name _____

W9-BOF-872

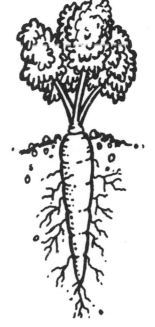

Slurp, slurp! On a hot summer day, a cherry soda is cool and refreshing. Plants like to drink too. The plant's root system slurps water and **minerals** from the ground.

There are **two** kinds of root systems. Some plants have one main root that grows deep into the ground. This is called a **tap** root. Other plants have shallow roots with many **branches**. These roots are called **fibrous** roots.

Attached to both root systems are tiny root **hairs** that do all the work of absorbing water.

Color the tap root orange. Color the fibrous roots brown. Write the name of the root system in the blank space. Label the root hairs.

Use the words in bold to complete the word puzzle. Then find the mystery word in the puzzle.

1. The _____ root grows deep into the ground.

2. Roots "slurp" water and _____.

3. Fibrous roots have many _____.

4. Tiny root _____ absorb water.

5. There are _____ types of root systems.

6. _____ roots grow shallow.

1. __ __ __
2. __ __ __ __ __ __ __ __
3. __ __ __ __ __ __ __ __
4. __ __ __ __ __
5. __ __ __ __
6. __ __ __ __ __ __ __

Use the mystery word in the puzzle to solve the riddle.

A ship's is made of iron,
To hold it fast at berth.
A plant's roots work like one,
To hold it firm in the earth.

What is it? _____

Fun Fact

The American Indians boiled the balsam root to make tea. They drank the tea when they had a sore throat, cough, pneumonia, or hay fever.

Tre-e-emendous Plant

Name _____

Word Bank
seed
trunk
leaves
roots
bark

What is the largest plant growing near your school? It is probably a tree. It may be a maple, oak, pine, or palm. All trees have many of the same parts as the plants that grow in your garden—only much larger.

The riddles tell about the jobs of the tree parts. Use the tree parts listed in the Word Bank to solve each riddle. Then label the parts of the tree.

Green and flat
Or needle-like,
We make food by day
And rest at night.

_____

From roots to branches,
Short or long,
My tough wood
Keeps me tall and strong.

_____

Scattered by wind
When breezes blow,
I'll make a new tree
When I sprout and grow.

_____

Thin-like hair,
Or thick and round,
We hold the tree
Firmly in the ground.

_____

Rough or smooth,
A very tough cover,
I keep out insects,
Fire, and weather.

_____

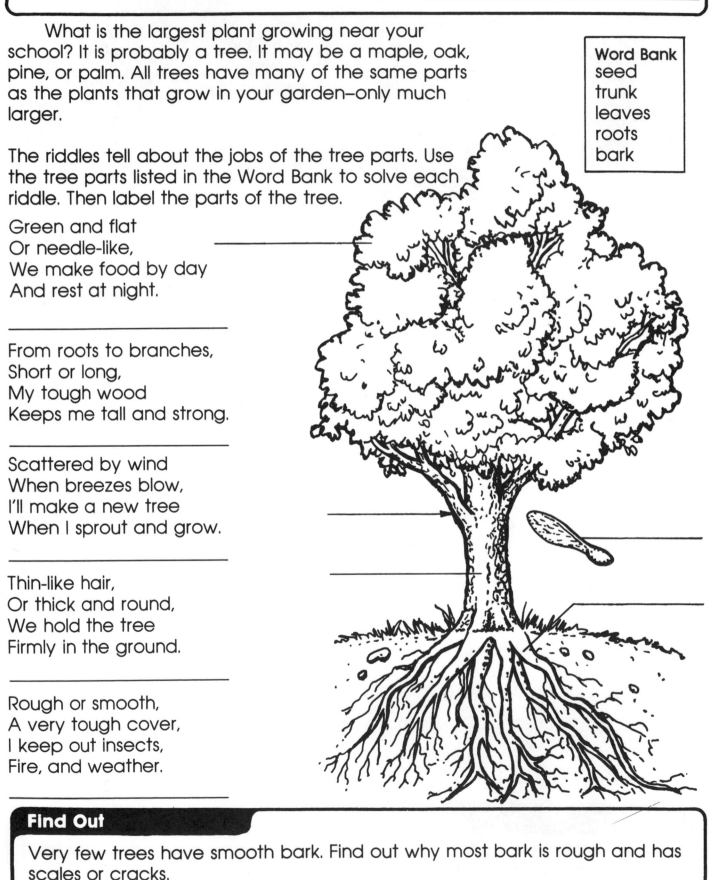

Find Out

Very few trees have smooth bark. Find out why most bark is rough and has scales or cracks.

Leaves or Needles

Name _____

Everyone has seen trees, but how do you tell one kind of tree from another? Trees have different leaves, seeds, bark, and flowers.

There are two main kinds of trees. The **conifers** are trees with needle-like leaves. Their seeds are found in cones. Conifers stay green all year long.

The **broad-leaved** trees have leaves of different sizes and shapes. Broad-leaved trees often lose their leaves in the fall. In warm regions, some broad-leaved trees keep their leaves all year long.

Find the hidden conifer trees in the conifer tree. Find the hidden broad-leaved trees in the broad-leaved tree. Use the word bank to help you.

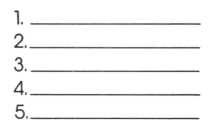
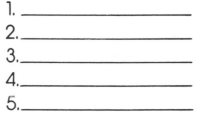

Word Bank

oak	ash
pine	elm
beech	spruce
redwood	cedar
fir	maple

1. _____   1. _____
2. _____   2. _____
3. _____   3. _____
4. _____   4. _____
5. _____   5. _____

Solve the word puzzle.

Down
1. Conifer leaves are shaped like

   _____.

Across
2. Conifers stay _____ all year long.

3. Broad-leaved trees lose their leaves in the _____.

4. Conifer seeds are in _____.

Something Special

Make a list of as many kinds of trees as you can think of. Circle the trees that grow in your state or province.

"Color-fall" Leaves

Name _____

Fill in the blanks with words from the Word Bank.

Some broad-leaved trees like the maple are very colorful in the _____. The beautiful reds, oranges, and yellows were always in the leaves. But their colors were hidden by the _____ during the spring and _____.

The green is _____. Chlorophyll is the matter in the _____ that makes food for the tree. When fall comes, the tree stops making food, and the green chlorophyll dies. As the green disappears, the beautiful colors of fall appear.

Complete the word puzzle using words from the Word Bank.

Find the hidden word in the puzzle. Use it to answer the riddle at the bottom.

1. Food is made in the _____.

2. Trees make food in the spring and _____.

3. Fall colors are hidden by the _____.

4. Leaves stop making food in the _____.

5. The green matter that makes food is _____.

1. __ __ __ __ __ __

2.   __ __ __ __ __

3.   __ __ __ __

4.   __ __ __ __

5.   __ __ __ __ __ __ __ __ __ __

Word Bank

chlorophyll	fall
green	leaves
summer	

Kids really like me,
I'm food for the trees.
My taste is really sweet,
And I'm made by the leaves.

What am I? _____

Something Special

Make rubbings of different kinds of leaves. Place a sheet of paper over a leaf. Gently rub the paper with the side of a crayon. Try overlapping rubbings and using different colors. Use the rubbings to decorate the cover of a booklet about leaves or a leaf collection.

Living History Books

Name _____

You can learn a lot about a tree by reading its special calendar of rings. Every year a tree grows a new layer of wood. This makes the tree trunk get fatter and fatter. The new layer makes a ring.

You can see the rings on a freshly cut tree stump. When the growing season is wet, the tree grows a lot and the rings are wide. When the season is dry, the tree grows very little. Then the rings are narrow.

This tree was planted in 1970. Use the picture clues to color the rings of the tree stump. Where will the very first ring be?

1970
The tree was planted. Color the ring green.

1985
The tree was cut down. Color the ring yellow.

?
The year you were born. Color the ring red.

1979
A very wet growing season. Color the ring blue.

1984
A very dry growing season. Color the ring brown.

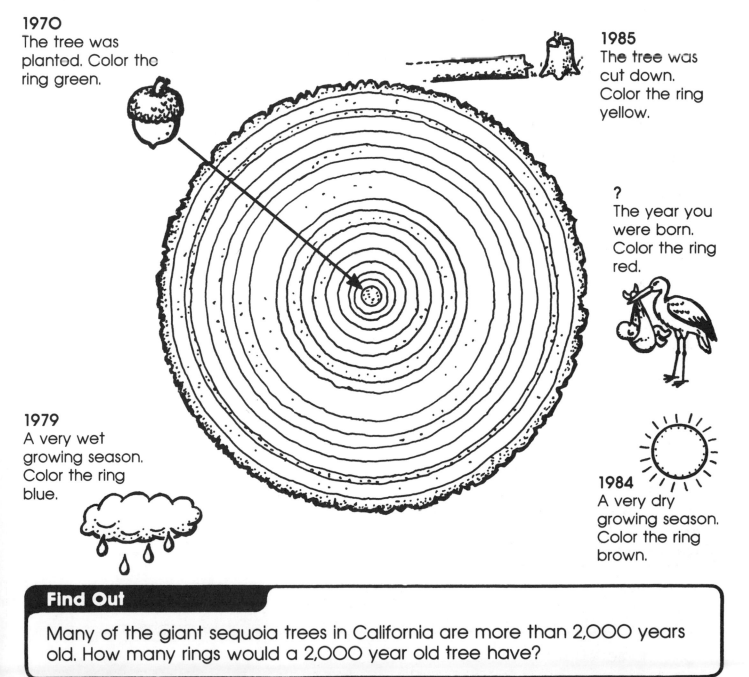

Find Out

Many of the giant sequoia trees in California are more than 2,000 years old. How many rings would a 2,000 year old tree have?

Plant Parts

Name _____

Green, flowering plants grow all around you. Beautiful red roses, tall corn-stalks, or prickly thistle weeds are all green, flowering plants. Green, flowering plants have six parts: stem, root, leaf, flower, fruit, and seed.

_____

_____

_____

_____

Complete the word puzzle. Then use the words from the puzzle to label the plant.

Across

1. I often have bright colors, but my real job is to make seeds.
3. I carry water from the roots to the leaves and food back to the roots.
4. I collect energy from the sun to make food for the plant.

Down

1. I often taste delicious, but my job is to hold and protect the seeds.
2. I hold the plant tight like an anchor, but also collect water and minerals from the soil.
3. Someday a new plant will grow from me.

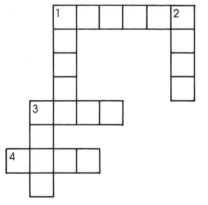

Fun Fact

The American Indians used every part of the sunflowers they grew. They ate the root and fed the stem and leaves to their animals. They ground the seeds for meal and used the yellow petals for dye. They even used the oil from the seeds for their hair.

Flower Power

Name _____

Flowers are beautiful to look at and pleasant to smell, but they also have a very important job. Most plants make seeds inside the flower.

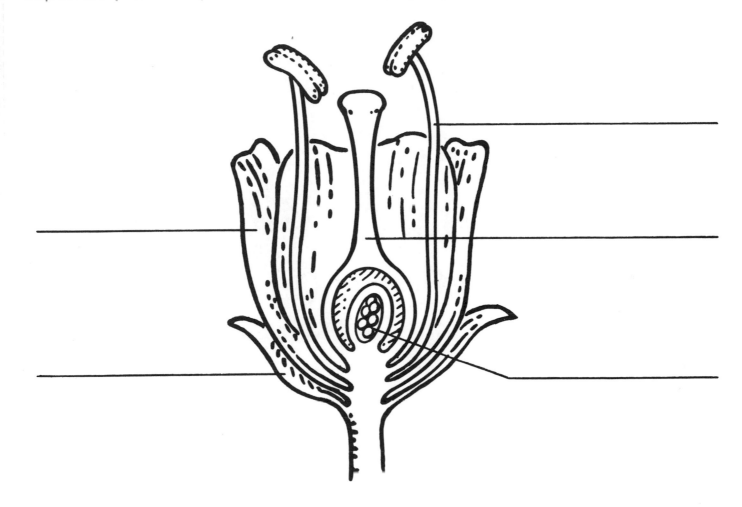

Color each flower part the color listed on the chart. Label each part.

Flower Part	Description	Color
pistil	A large center stalk, often shaped like a water bottle.	yellow
stamen	A tall, thin stalk with a knobbed tip. It holds grains of pollen.	brown
petal	Brightly colored and sweet-smelling leaves.	red
sepal	Small leaf-like part at the base of the flower.	green
ovary	Ball-shaped part at the base of the pistil. This is where the seeds develop.	blue

Garden Fresh Produce

Name _____

Plants give us all the fruits, vegetables, grains, spices, and herbs we eat. Amy has just planted her garden. List all of the fruits and vegetables in Amy's garden under the correct plant part that can be eaten.

Stem

_____

_____

Leaf

_____

_____

Flower

_____

_____

Root

_____

_____

Fruit

_____

_____

Seed

_____

_____

Bulb

_____

_____

Amy's garden has only a few of the many, many kinds of fruits and vegetables. Make a chart like the one below. Complete the chart with as many kinds of fruits and vegetables as you can name. Circle the ones you like to eat. Put a "?" in front of the ones you have never tasted.

Vegetable or Fruit	Root	Stem	Leaf	Flower	Bulb	Fruit	Seed
kiwi						✓	

Dirty Work

Name _____

"Matt, please wash your dirty hands!" Soil does more than just make your hands dirty. It is important for making plants grow.

Soil is made of **rock, humus, air,** and **water.** The rock is often in the form of sand or clay. Sand Is easy to dig, but it doesn't hold water. Clay holds water, but is packed too tightly to let plants grow. Humus is matter that was once alive, but now it is decayed or rotted. Humus gives nutrients to the soil. Plants need nutrients to grow.

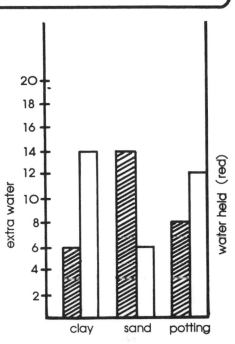

Matt's Experiment

Matt wanted to find out how much water three kinds of soil would hold. He tested clay, sand, and potting soil. (Potting soil is a mixture of clay, sand, and humus.) Matt took three baby food jars and filled each one half-way with one of the soils. Then he poured 20 cc of water into each one. After mixing each jar of soil and water, he poured off the extra water. Matt measured the extra water.

Look at the graph to see his results.

1. Which soil had the most extra water? _____
2. Which soil had the least extra water?_____
3. To find how much water each soil held, you must subtract the extra water from 20cc. Look at the example and then find out how much water each of the other two soils held.

    Clay: 20 cc – 6 cc = 14 cc of water held

    Sand: 20 cc – _____ = _____ cc of water held

    Potting: 20 cc – _____ = _____ cc of water held

4. Draw your results of the "water held" for each soil on Matt's chart. Use a red crayon or marker.
5. Which soil had the most nutrients? _____
6. Which soil would you use for planting? _____

    Why? _____

Something Special

Try Matt's experiment on your own. Compare your results.

Light Work

Name _____

Leaves work like little factories making food for the plant. There is a **green** material called **chlorophyll** in each leaf. Chlorophyll is like a little "green machine" changing **water** and air into food. Like most machines, this machine needs energy to work. The green machine gets its energy from **sunlight.** Without sunlight, the **leaves** could not make food.

Amy and Matt both received healthy, potted flowers. Amy kept her plant in a bright, sunny window. Matt kept his in a dark corner of his room.

What happened to Amy's plant?

_____

What happened to Matt's plant?

_____

Amy's Plant   Matt's Plant

Complete the sentences using the words in bold from above. Use the numbered letters to answer the mystery question.

1. Food-making material in leaves is called __ __ __ __ __ __ __ __ __ __ .
   <small>3   1 2 7</small>

2. Plants make food from air and __ __ __ __ __ .
   <small>4</small>

3. The green machine gets its energy from __ __ __ __ __ __ __ __ .
   <small>8   9</small>

4. Food is made in the plant's __ __ __ __ __ __ .
   <small>6</small>

5. The color of chlorophyll is __ __ __ __ __ .
   <small>5</small>

Mystery Question
What is the scientific name for the process of making food with the help of light?

__ __ __ __ __ __ __ __ __ __ __ __ __
<small>1 2 3 4 3 6 7 8 4 2 5 6 9 6</small>

Find Out

What do we call the food that is made by the leaves?

Cruising Coconuts

Name _____

"Look at this coconut!" Amy called to Matt as they walked along the beach. Safe inside its thick husk, the coconut had floated across the water. Once it washed up on shore, the green leaves sprouted from this large seed.

Seeds travel in many ways. Below are five ways that seeds travel. Tell how each seed travels.

_____
_____
_____
_____
_____
_____
_____
_____
_____
_____
_____
_____
_____
_____
_____
_____
_____
_____

Fun Fact

Blast Off
The seed pod of the "touch-me-not" swells as it gets ripe. Finally the seed pod bursts and launches seeds in all directions.

Jogging Geraniums

Name _____

You will probably never see a flower running down the sidewalk, but you might see one climbing a fence. Most plants are rooted in one place, but they still move.

Roots, stems, leaves, and even flowers move in different ways. The leaves grow toward the light. Roots will grow toward water. Even gravity will make a plant grow straight up in the air, away from the center of the earth.

Look at the three plants below. Tell what made the plants "move" or grow the way they did.

_____   _____   _____

_____   _____   _____

_____   _____   _____

Scientists gives special names to the three kinds of plant movements above. The names come from combining two words. Put the correct puzzle pieces together to make the new word. Write the new word. Label the pictures above with the correct new word.

	New Word	Meaning
photo "light" + tropism "turn"	_____	To turn toward the light.
geo "earth" + tropism "turn"	_____	To turn because of of earth's gravity.
hydro "water" + tropism "turn"	_____	To turn toward the water.

©1992 Instructional Fair, Inc.   IF8758 Science Enrichment

Corny Medicine

Name _____

Use the words from the Word Bank to complete the puzzle. Cross out each word in the Word Bank as you use it. The remaining words in the Word Bank will help you answer the "Corny Medicine" riddle.

Across
4. Deep growing type of root
6. Beautiful, seed-making part of plant
7. Brightly colored "leafy" parts of the flower
9. Large part of seed that supplies food
10. Sweet food made by the leaves

Down
1. Making food with the help of light
2. Green food-making material in a leaf
3. Plant's "food factory"
5. Plant's anchor
8. Plants get their energy from the

_____.

Corny Medicine
Why did the cornstalk go to the doctor's office?

_____

Word Bank				
petals	because	cotyledon	it	root
had	flower	leaf	an	sugar
chlorophyll	sun	photosynthesis	ear	tap
ache				

Living Things

Name _____

Look at the many living things on this page. A scientist calls these and any other living things **organisms.** Many organisms are alike in some way. They can be put into groups according to the ways they are alike. Putting organisms into groups is called **classifying.**

Classifying

1. Sort the organisms pictured above into two groups. Color all of the organisms in one group. Leave the other group plain. How are all of the organisms in the colored group alike?

   _____

   How are all of the organisms in the uncolored group alike?

   _____

2. Find the ten organisms hidden in the wordsearch. They belong in one of the groups. Unscramble the group names and list the organisms under the correct group heading.

```
C A R R O T U B
O F A F E A D T
R O B I N S O J
N A B E D U G M
O F I H R O C O
H E T R E E L U
U R I G R A S S
I N S E C T H E
```

tlanp_____   limaan _____

1. _____   1. _____
2. _____   2. _____
3. _____   3. _____
4. _____   4. _____
5. _____   5. _____

Fun Fact

There are more than 700,000 kinds, or **species,** of insects in the world. This is more than all the other species of animals grouped together.

©1992 Instructional Fair, Inc.   14   IF8758 Science Enrichment

Backbone or No Backbone?

Name _____

Which part of your body helps you stand tall or sit up straight? It is your backbone. You are a member of a large group of animals that all have backbones. Animals with backbones are called **vertebrates.** Birds, fish, reptiles, amphibians, and mammals are all vertebrates.

Some animals do not have backbones. These animals are called **invertebrates.** Worms, centipedes, and insects are all invertebrates.

Classifying

Find the five vertebrates and five invertebrates hidden in the wordsearch. Then write them in the correct group.

Invertebrates

1. _____
2. _____
3. _____
4. _____
5. _____

```
B R A B B I T B U D
E A G I R A F F E L
E W O F H E P R U W
T O G K L C M O T H
L R N F R Y S G I A
E M L I O N O J E L
R S P I D E R M R E
```

Vertebrates

1. _____
2. _____
3. _____
4. _____
5. _____

Your neighborhood has many animals in or near it. Add their names to the lists.

Invertebrates

6. _____
7. _____
8. _____
9. _____
10. _____

Vertebrates

6. _____
7. _____
8. _____
9. _____
10. _____

Find Out

There are many more invertebrates than vertebrates. Nine out of ten animals is an invertebrate. Which group has the largest animals? Which group has the smallest animals?

Six-Legged Friends

Name _____

The largest group of animals belongs to the group called invertebrates–or animals without backbones. This large group is the **insect** group.

Insects are easy to tell apart from other animals. Adult insects have three body parts and six legs. The first body part is the **head.** On the head are the mouth, eyes, and antennae. The second body part is the **thorax.** On it are the legs and wings. The third part is the **abdomen.** On it are small openings for breathing.

Color the body parts of the insect above. head–red, thorax–yellow, abdomen–blue

Draw an insect below. Make your insect a one-of-a-kind. Be sure it has the correct number of body parts, legs, wings, and antennae. Fill in the information.

Insect's name_____   Warning: _____

Length _____   _____

Where found _____   _____

Food_____   _____

Find Out

Many people think that spiders are insects. Spiders and insects are alike in many ways, but spiders are not insects. Find out how the two are different.

Flutterby or Butterfly

Name _____

Have you ever seen a butterfly "flutterby" on a warm summer day?

Use the words from the word bank to complete the story of the life cycle of the butterfly and the moth.

The butterfly and the __ __ __ __ go through a special change during their life cycle. They begin life as a tiny __ __ __. The egg hatches
into a hungry __ __ __ __ __ __ __ __ __ __ __. After eating large amounts of
__ __ __ __, the caterpillar is ready for an amazing change. The butterfly
caterpillar forms a __ __ __ __ __ __ __ __ __. The moth caterpillar spins a
__ __ __ __ __ __ out of __ __ __ __ thread. While in the cocoon or chrysalis, the
caterpillar changes into an __ __ __ __ __. A few weeks later, the adult butterfly
and the adult moth will emerge.

(numbered spaces: 1 under "They"; 2, 7 under the long blank for "caterpillar"; 5 under "food"; 8, 6 under second blank; 9 under "cocoon"; 10, 11 under "silk"; 4, 3 under "adult")

Use the letters from the numbered spaces above to find the name of the life cycle of the butterfly and the moth.

__ __ __ __ __ __ __ __ __ __ __ __
1 2 3 4 1 5 6 7 8 9 10 11 10

It's not difficult to tell a butterfly from a moth. Study the pictures. Write **M** or **B** before each clue.

____ furry antennae   ____ flies at night

____ knobbed antennae   ____ flies during day

____ fatter body   ____ brightly colored

____ forms chrysalis   ____ forms cocoon

Word Bank	
chrysalis	food
adult	silk
moth	cocoon
caterpillar	egg

Fun Fact

The male emperor moth has the sharpest sense of smell of all animals. It can smell the scent of the female emperor moth from 11 km away.

Frog's Life Cycle

Name _____

The frog goes through many changes during its life. Read about the frog's life cycle below. Then complete the word puzzle using what you have learned.

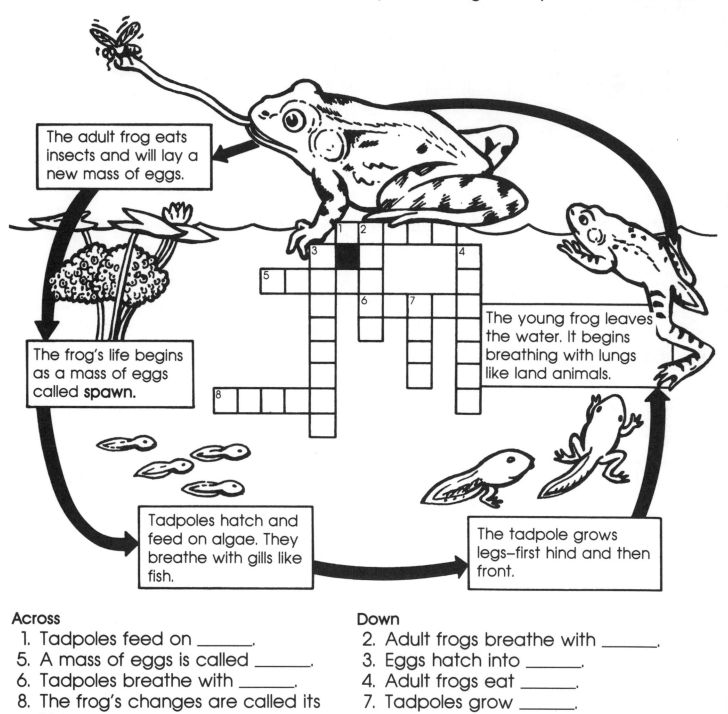

The adult frog eats insects and will lay a new mass of eggs.

The frog's life begins as a mass of eggs called **spawn**.

The young frog leaves the water. It begins breathing with lungs like land animals.

Tadpoles hatch and feed on algae. They breathe with gills like fish.

The tadpole grows legs—first hind and then front.

Across

1. Tadpoles feed on _____.
5. A mass of eggs is called _____.
6. Tadpoles breathe with _____.
8. The frog's changes are called its life _____.

Down

2. Adult frogs breathe with _____.
3. Eggs hatch into _____.
4. Adult frogs eat _____.
7. Tadpoles grow _____.

Find Out

In many areas, ponds and streams freeze in the winter. What happens to the frogs that live in the pond?

Going Places

Looking at a bird's feet can tell you a lot about how they are used. Look at the bird's feet below. Unscramble the bird's name. Write the bird's name by the best sentence. Can you match the pictures with the names?

kawh

noreh

_____
ckud

_____
reckwoodep

_____ "My webbed feet are great for swimming."

_____ "My feet are great for walking up trees."

_____ "I use my feet with long toes to wade in the water and mud."

_____ "I use my strong, powerful feet to catch small animals."

Can the shape of a bird's bill tell you anything about what it eats? Look closely at the bills below. Unscramble the bird's name. Write the bird's name by the best sentence. Can you match the pictures with the names?

noreh

reckwoodep

_____
bumminghird

_____
kawh

_____
panicel

_____
dinalcar

_____ "I pound holes in wood to find insects."

_____ "I use my long bill to get nectar from flowers."

_____ "I use my strong bill to crack open seeds."

_____ "I use my sharp bill to tear the flesh of animals."

_____ "I stab at small fish with my sharp bill."

_____ "I scoop up large mouthfuls of water and fish."

Feathered Friend

Make your own feathered friend. Color, cut out, and paste this bird together on another sheet of paper. Write a short paragraph that tells where your new bird lives, what it eats, and what its living habits are.

legs

tails

wings

bills

"Oh my, how you have grown!"

Name _____

"My swimsuit doesn't fit. It fit me fine last summer." Surprise! You're growing!

What makes your body grow? Your body is made up of about 50 trillion cells. One of the most important jobs of a cell is to make you grow. One cell divides and forms two cells. Two cells divide and form four cells, and so on.

Not all of your cells keep dividing. Some cells die. But don't worry. Other cells are dividing and replacing those that died. There are even a few left over to help you grow.

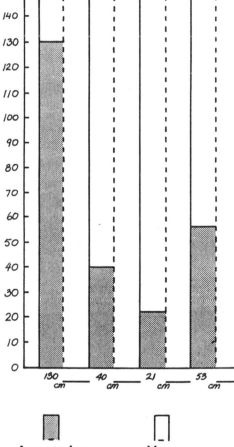

Amanda kept a record of her growth. You can take your own measurements too. Then fill in the chart and compare your growth with Amanda's growth. You may need a friend to help you.

1. Who is taller, Amanda or you? _____

   By how many centimeters? _____

2. Measure your arms from your shoulder to your wrist.

   Who has longer arms? _____

   By how many centimeters? _____

3. What makes your body grow? _____

   _____

Amanda   You

Personal History

Ask your parents what your height and weight were when you were born.

How much have you grown? _____

Fun Facts

Your fastest growing stage happened before you were born. During the first week, when you were first inside your mother, you grew from one cell into billions of cells!

Body Building Blocks

Name _____

Just like some houses are built with bricks, your body is built with cells. Every part of your body is made of cells.

Cells differ in **size** and **shape,** but they all have a few things in common. All cells have a nucleus. The **nucleus** is the center of the cell. It controls the cell's activities. Cells can **divide** and become two cells exactly like the original cell.

Your body has many kinds of cells. Each kind has a special job. **Muscle** cells help you move. Nerve cells carry messages between your brain and other parts of your body. Blood cells carry **oxygen** to other cells in your body.

Complete each sentence using the words in bold from above.

The __ __ __ __ __ __ __ controls the cell's
    3
activities.

Cells differ in __ __ __ __ and __ __ __ __ __.
           2   1

One cell can __ __ __ __ __ __ into two cells.
                6

__ __ __ __ __ __ cells help you move.
      5

Blood cells carry __ __ __ __ __ __ to other
cells in your body.   4

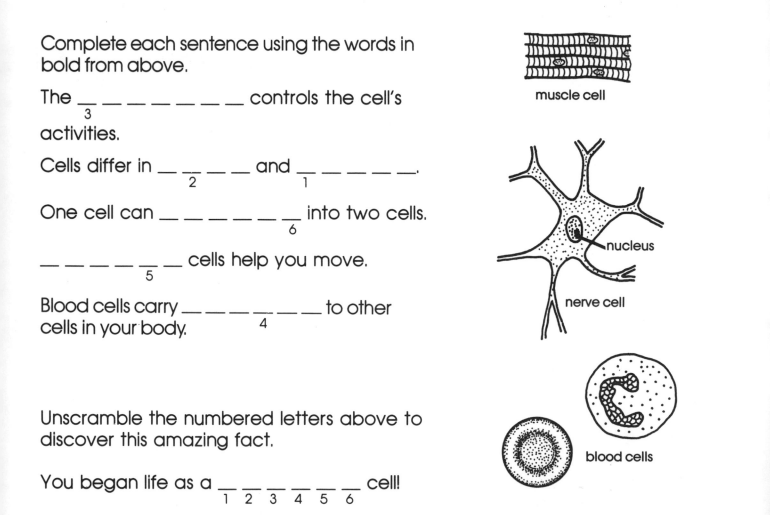

muscle cell

nucleus

nerve cell

blood cells

Unscramble the numbered letters above to discover this amazing fact.

You began life as a __ __ __ __ __ __ cell!
            1 2 3 4 5 6

Fun Facts

People and most animals are made of billions or even trillions of cells. But some animals are made of only one cell. To find out more about these animals, look up "protozoans" in your library.

©1992 Instructional Fair, Inc. IF8758 Science Enrichment

Framework

Name _____

What gives you your **shape?** Like a house's frame, your body also has a frame. It is called your **skeleton.** Your skeleton is made of more than two hundred bones.

Your skeleton helps your body move. It does this by giving your **muscles** a place to attach. Your skeleton also **protects** the soft organs inside your body from injury.

Bones have a hard, outer layer made of **calcium.** Inside each bone is a soft, **spongy** layer that looks like a honeycomb. The hollow spaces in the honeycomb are filled with **marrow.** Every minute, millions of **blood** cells die. But you don't need to worry. The bone marrow works like a little factory, making new blood cells for you.

Use the words in bold to finish the sentences.

1. Your skeleton __ __ __ __ __ __ __ __ your soft organs.
    5

2. Bone __ __ __ __ __ __ makes new blood cells.
       2

3. Inside the bone is a soft, __ __ __ __ __ __ layer.
                                      3

4. Millions of __ __ __ __ __ cells die every minute.
             4

5. The hard, outer layer of bone is made from __ __ __ __ __ __ __.
                                                     1

6. More than two hundred bones are in your __ __ __ __ __ __ __ __.
                                                              6

7. Your skeleton is a place for __ __ __ __ __ __ __ to attach.
                                            7

8. Your skeleton gives your body its __ __ __ __ __.
                                            8

Something Special

What do you call a skeleton that won't get out of bed? Use the numbered letters above to find out.

__ __ __z__ __ __ __ __ __ __
 1 2   3 4 5 6 7 8

©1992 Instructional Fair, Inc.   29   IF8758 Science Enrichment

Incredible Journey

Name _____

Put on your hard hat. Lower the rope. Let's find out what happened to that apple Fred just ate.

The first 8 cm of rope takes us through Fred's **mouth.** Those big teeth grind his food. The liquid around us, called saliva, helps break down the food and makes swallowing easier.

The next 42 cm we lower ourselves down a long tube called the **esophagus.** Hold on tight! We are entering the **stomach.** There is a lot of mixing and churning for the next 20 cm. The food is breaking down more and becoming very soupy.

Now comes a long, curly 640 cm through the **small intestine.** Here, the food is broken down into nutrients. The nutrients pass into the bloodstream through the intestinal wall. The last part of our journey is 150 cm through the **large intestine.** The waste leaves the body through the opening at the end of the large intestine, called the **anus.**

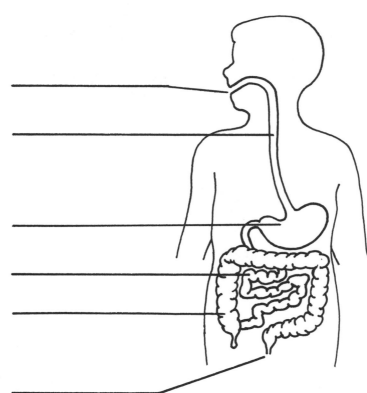

1. Label the parts of Fred's digestive system using the words in bold from above.

2. What is the total length of the digestive system ? _____

3. Why is it important to chew your food well?_____

_____

4. What happens to the nutrients in your food? _____

_____

Find Out

The average person eats more than 450 kg. of food each year. Why don't you gain 450 kg. in weight each year?

Breathing Tree

Did you know that you have a tree inside your chest? This tree has a special job. It takes air from your windpipe and spreads it all through your lungs. This tree is called your **bronchial tree.**

Air enters through your **nose.** It passes over the hairs inside your nose. This warms and cleanses the air. Then it travels down your **windpipe** until it comes to your bronchial tree. The bronchial tree divides into two tubes. One tube sends air into your right **lung.** The other tube sends air into your left lung.

Inside the lungs, the air fills almost 300 million tiny, spongy **air sacs.** These air sacs give fresh **oxygen** to the blood. At the same time, they take away **carbon dioxide** from the blood. Carbon dioxide is the air that has already been used. When you exhale, the carbon dioxide flows up the bronchial tree and out of your mouth and nose.

The nose, windpipe, bronchial tree, lungs, and air sacs work as a team. The team is called the **respiratory system.**

Label the parts of the respiratory system.

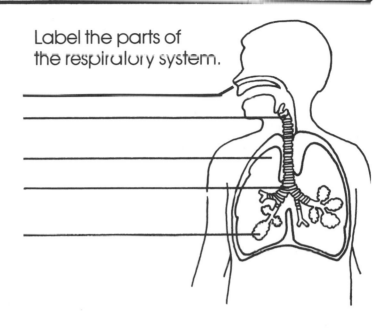

Who am I?

Inhale these scrambled words. Exhale the answers to the riddles.

1. I warm and clean the air you breathe. SNOE _____

2. There are 300 million of me in your lungs. RAI SCAS _____

3. You breathe me out. RONBAC DOXEIDI _____

4. I am your special tree. CHONRBALI REET _____

5. I am a long tube connecting your mouth to your lungs. DINWIPPE _____

6. I go through the air sacs and into the blood. YXONEG _____

Find Out

Smoking is harmful to your lungs. How can smoking affect breathing?

Blood Work

Name _____

If you could look at a drop of your blood under a microscope, you would see some odd-shaped cells floating around in a liquid called **plasma.** These are the **white blood cells.** White blood cells are "soldiers" that fight germs which cause disease.

You would also see many smaller, saucer-shaped cells called **red blood cells.** Red blood cells give your blood its red color. They also have the important job of carrying **oxygen** to all of the cells in your body.

Blood **platelets** go to work when you have a cut. They form a plug, called a clot, that stops the bleeding.

Blood travels throughout your whole body. It goes to the **lungs** to get oxygen and to the intestines to get digested food. It carries the oxygen and food nutrients to all parts of your body. It also takes away carbon dioxide and other waste products.

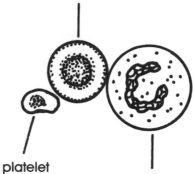

red blood cell

platelet

white blood cell

Fill in the spaces with words from the word bank.

1. Red blood cells carry __ __ __ __ __ __.
                                    5

2. The blood gets oxygen from your __ __ __ __ __.
                                          4

3. Blood carries __ __ __ __ nutrients from the intestines.

4. __ __ __ __ __ blood cells fight germs.
       2

5. Blood travels to all parts of your __ __ __ __.
                                           6

6. The liquid part of the blood is called __ __ __ __ __ __.
                                                 7

7. __ __ __ blood cells give blood its color.
     3

8. __ __ __ __ __ __ __ __ __ form blood clots.

9. Adults donate blood at a blood __ __ __ __.
                                      1

Word Bank

oxygen
platelets
red
white
bank
lungs
plasma
food
body

Something Special

Use the numbered letters to finish the sentence. "Dirty" blood is cleansed by two large bean-shaped organs. These organs are called __ __ __ __ __ __ __.
                                                                                              1 2 3 4 5 6 7

Your Body's Pipeline

Name _____

Blood travels through three kinds of tubes. **Arteries** carry oxygen-rich blood from your heart to other parts of your body. Blood vessels, called **veins,** carry carbon dioxide-rich blood back to your heart. **Capillaries** are tiny vessels that connect arteries and veins. Capillaries take carbon dioxide from the cells and give the cells oxygen. Capillaries are fifty times thinner than a hair. They are so small that the blood cells must line up one at a time to travel through them.

Your heart, blood, arteries, veins, and capillaries work as a team. This team is called your **circulatory system.**

Name three kinds of blood vessels.

_____

_____

_____

The picture shows your circulatory system. Color the veins blue. Color the arteries red. Color the heart brown.

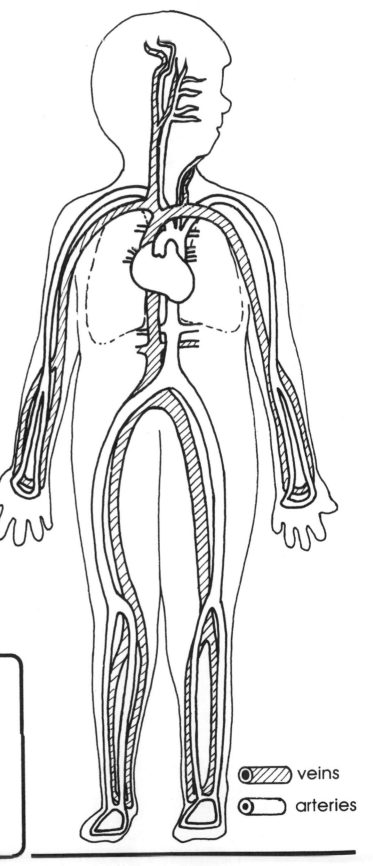

veins

arteries

Fun Facts

With every beat of your heart, blood starts a fantastic journey. Your blood travels through 96,000 km of blood vessels to all the cells in your body.

©1992 Instructional Fair, Inc.

IF8758 Science Enrichment

Lub-Dub, Lub-Dub

Name _____

Place your hand on the left side of your chest. Lub-dub, lub-dub. Did you feel it? This is your heart pumping oxygen-rich blood to all parts of your body.

Your heart is really two pumps. It is divided down the middle. Each half of the heart is divided into two chambers. The **right half** pumps blood filled with a waste called carbon dioxide gas into the lungs. The **left half** of the heart takes oxygen-rich blood from the lungs. It sends the oxygen-rich blood to the cells in your body.

What about lub-dub? These are the sounds made by the little "trap doors" called **valves**. The valves open and close to let the blood flow in and out of the heart.

Blood to the Lungs

Blood to the Body

Blood from the Lungs

Blood to the Lungs

Blood from the Lungs

The arrows show the direction of blood flowing through the heart.

1. How many pumps does your heart have? _____

2. Where does the right half pump its blood? _____

3. Where does the left half pump its blood? _____

4. Which part of the heart makes the lub-dub sound? _____

Something Special

You can actually feel your heart at work, pumping blood through your body, by pressing on one of your arteries. This is called "taking your pulse." Your teacher can show you how to take your pulse. Take your pulse after each activity to find out how hard your heart works.

Activity	Pulse Rate
jumping	_____
sitting	_____

1. During which activity was your pulse the slowest? _____

2. During which activity was your pulse the fastest? _____

3. Why do you think your pulse rate increased? _____

Think Tank

Name _____

Your brain has a very important job. It must keep your body working smoothly all day and night.

Your brain has three parts. The **cerebrum** is the largest part. It controls your body movements, such as running, walking, jumping, throwing a ball, holding a fork, and other actions. It controls your five senses: hearing, smelling, tasting, seeing, and touching. The cerebrum also controls your thinking and speaking.

The cerebrum is divided into two halves. The right half controls movements in the left side of your body. The left half controls movements in the right side of your body.

The part below the cerebrum is the **cerebellum.** The cerebellum makes sure that all of your muscles work together the way they are supposed to. It also helps you keep your balance.

The third and smallest part of the brain is the **brain stem.** The brain stem's job is extremely important. It controls breathing and the beating of your heart.

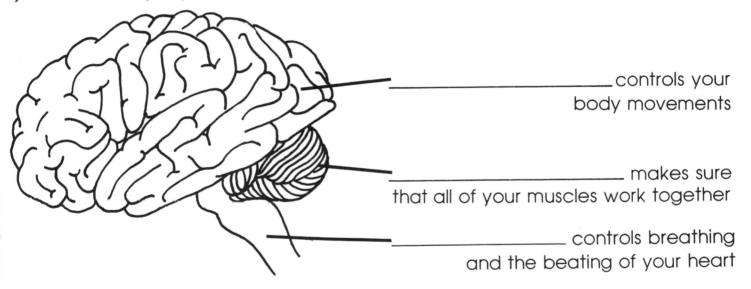

_____ controls your body movements

_____ makes sure that all of your muscles work together

_____ controls breathing and the beating of your heart

Label the three major parts of the brain.

Which part of the skeleton protects the brain from injury? Give the common name and the scientific name. (Hint: Billy Bones can help with this one.)

common name: _____ scientific name: _____

Fun Facts

In order to function properly, the brain must have a constant supply of blood. The blood provides oxygen and other vitamins and nutrients needed by the brain to stay healthy.

©1992 Instructional Fair, Inc. 35 IF8758 Science Enrichment

Your Body's Messenger Service

Name _____

Did you know that your nervous system has its own messenger service? Billions of tiny nerve cells throughout your body send messages to your brain.

First, the tiny nerve cells send their message to the spinal cord. (The spinal cord is a thick bundle of nerves running down the middle of your back.) Next, the spinal cord carries the message to your brain. Your brain reads the message and sends a new message back to your muscles. The new message tells your muscles how to move.

Think Fast!

How fast do you react to brain messages? Place your hand flat on the desk. Have a friend hold an eraser about 30 cm above your hand. Try to pull your hand away before your friend can drop the eraser on your hand.

Try five times and record each result. Put a (✓) in either the "hit" or "miss" box.

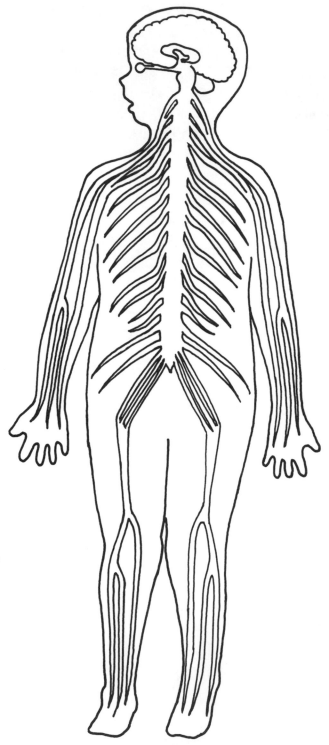

	#1	#2	#3	#4	#5
Hit					
Miss					

Color the parts of the nervous system.
    brain - gray
    spinal cord - blue   nerves - red

Find Out

What are some occupations that require a quick reaction time?

Windows

Name _____

"Oh, what beautiful brown eyes you have!" Whether you know it or not, those eyes are not totally brown. Only the iris is colored brown.

Your eye is shaped like a ball. It has a clear, round window in front called the **cornea.** The colored **iris** controls the amount of light that enters the eye. Light enters through an opening called the **pupil.** In bright light, your pupil is a small dot. In dim light, it is much larger. Behind the pupil is the **lens.** It focuses the light onto the back wall of your eye. This back wall is called the **retina.** The retina changes the light into nerve messages. These messages are sent to the brain along the **optic nerve.** Close your eyes. Gently touch them. They are firm because they are filled with a clear jelly called vitreous humor.

Label the parts of the eye using the words in bold from above.

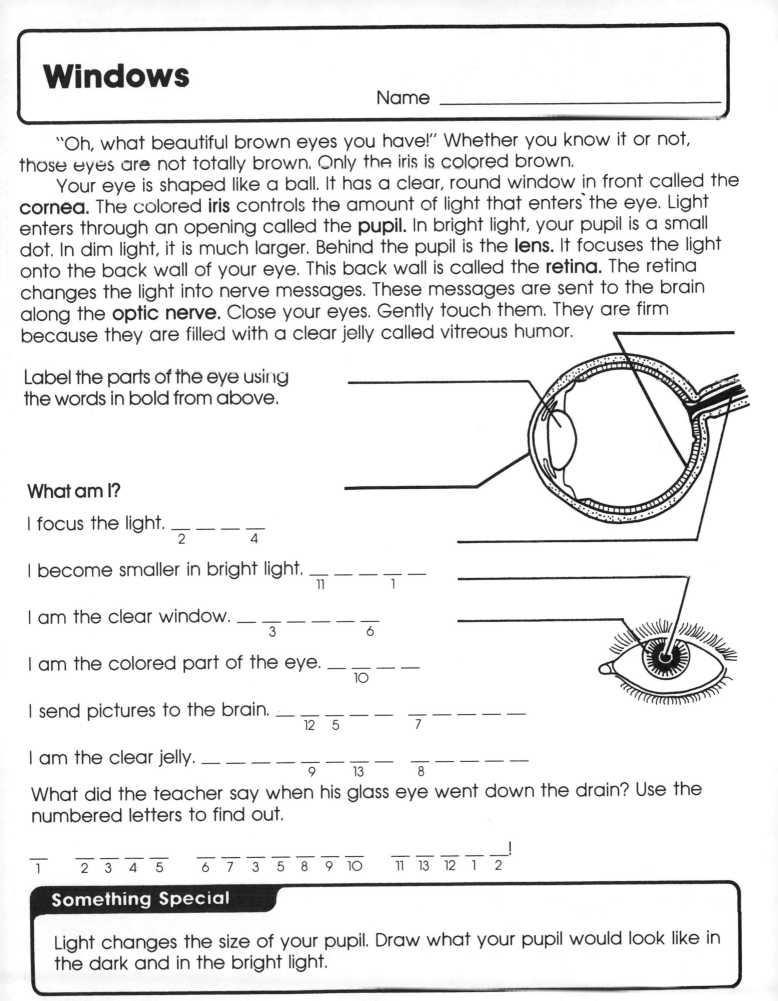

What am I?

I focus the light. __ __ __ __
　　　　　　　　2　　4

I become smaller in bright light. __ __ __ __ __
　　　　　　　　　　　　　　11　　　1

I am the clear window. __ __ __ __ __ __
　　　　　　　　　3　　　　6

I am the colored part of the eye. __ __ __ __
　　　　　　　　　　　　　10

I send pictures to the brain. __ __ __ __ __ __ __ __ __ __
　　　　　　　　　　　12 5　　　7

I am the clear jelly. __ __ __ __ __ __ __ __ __ __ __ __
　　　　　　　　　　　　9　　13　　8

What did the teacher say when his glass eye went down the drain? Use the numbered letters to find out.

__ __ __ __ __ __ __ __ __ __ __ __ __ __ __ __ __ __!
1　 2 3 4 5　 6 7 3 5 8 9 10　 11 13 12 1 2

Something Special

Light changes the size of your pupil. Draw what your pupil would look like in the dark and in the bright light.

Mouth Full of Teeth

Name _____

The boy in the picture has two sets of teeth. You do too!

Your first set are baby teeth that come in your first two years. When you are young, your jaw is small. It has just enough room for the twenty baby teeth. As you grow older, your jaw becomes larger. The thirty-two permanent teeth begin pushing on the baby teeth. Out fall the baby teeth.

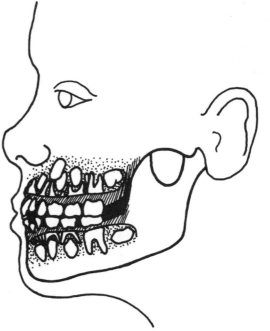

Taking good care of your teeth will help them last a lifetime. Sticky, chewy food sticks to your teeth. Germs in your mouth change these foods—especially sugar—into acid. The acid can eat holes, or cavities, in your teeth. Brushing or flossing your teeth removes the food and acid, helping to prevent cavities.

1. What are at least two things you can do to have healthy teeth?

_____

2. It is easy to brush at home. What can you do after eating your lunch at school to

keep your teeth clean? _____

Sweet, gooey foods are tooth destroyers. But some foods keep your teeth clean and slick. List tooth destroyers and tooth savers.

Tooth Destroyers _____   **Tooth Savers** _____

_____   _____

_____   _____

_____   _____

Find Out

Lyle says, "Why should I brush my baby teeth? They will just fall out anyway. I will take care of my permanent teeth when they come in." Is this a good idea? Why or why not?

Sound Collectors

Name _____

A large jet plane rumbles as it takes off down the runway. You can feel the ground vibrate. The plane is also filling the air with vibrations. When the vibrations reach your ear, you hear them as sound.

Your **outer ear** collects the vibrations just like a funnel. The vibrations strike your **eardrum,** making it vibrate too. These vibrations are passed through a series of three small bones. The last bone vibrates against a snail-shaped tube. This tube is called the **cochlea.** It is filled with liquid. Small hair-like sensors in the cochlea pick up the vibrations and send it to the **auditory nerve.** The auditory nerve sends the sound message to your brain.

Label the parts of the ear using the words in bold.

Sounds Around Us

1. What is the loudest sound you have ever heard? _____

2. What is the softest sound you have ever heard? _____

3. What sound wakes you up in the morning? _____

4. What sound relaxes you? _____

5. What sound frightens you? _____

Something Special

Try some of these sound experiments with your classmates. Keep your eyes closed for all of the experiments!
1. Cover one ear and listen for the sounds around you. Then uncover your ear and listen again. What is the difference?
2. Choose one student to make several sounds with objects found in the classroom. Can the rest of you identify the sounds?
3. We usually hear the loudest sounds around us. Listen for the soft, "far away" sounds. List the sounds. Try this experiment outside.

Yum-Yum

Name _____

Without the sense of taste, many things in life would not be as pleasant. What would it be like if all of your favorite foods had no taste at all?

Your sense of taste is found mainly in the tiny **tastebuds** on your tongue. To taste food, it must be chewed and mixed with **saliva**. The taste message is sent to the brain by nerves.

Each of the four tastes has a special center on the tongue. In each center, one of the main tastes is tasted more strongly.

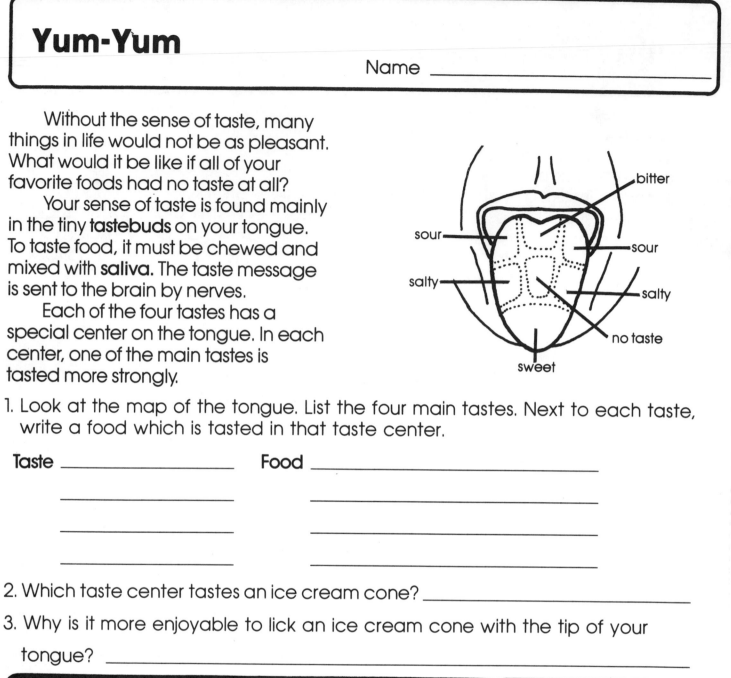

1. Look at the map of the tongue. List the four main tastes. Next to each taste, write a food which is tasted in that taste center.

Taste _____   Food _____

_____   _____

_____   _____

_____   _____

2. Which taste center tastes an ice cream cone? _____

3. Why is it more enjoyable to lick an ice cream cone with the tip of your

tongue? _____

Something Special

Where will each of these foods be tasted most strongly? Draw a line from the symbol for each food to its taste center on the tongue.

candy

vinegar

saltine cracker

lemon

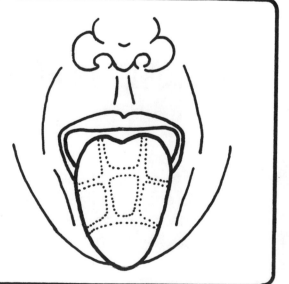

Peanut Butter and Sardine Sandwich

Name _____

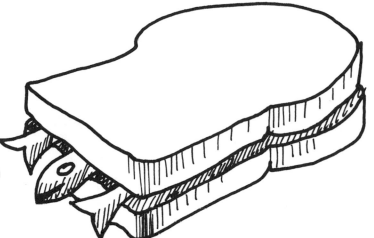

Your idea of a good meal may not be a peanut butter and sardine sandwich. But you do have a favorite food. Everyone does. Eating would be boring if we didn't have some favorites.

Let's make a chart. First, list your seven favorite foods. Then complete the chart by placing a check (✓) in the correct column(s).

Favorite Foods	Top Three Favorites	Snack Food	Prepare by Myself	Eat in a Restaurant	Ethnic Food
1.					
2.					
3.					
4.					
5.					
6.					
7.					

Compare your chart with your classmates' charts.

Something Special

ROYAL FEAST
You are the ruler for the day and may eat anything you want. Write a menu for today's royal feast.

Royal Menu

_____
_____
_____
_____
_____
_____
_____
_____
_____

You are what you eat.

Name _____

You are not made out of pickles and carrots. The food you eat must be digested before your body can use it. Digested food is changed into nutrients which help your body grow and give you energy.

Unscramble the names of the six nutrient groups. Use the word bank.

netroips _____

ralmenis _____

afts _____

ratew _____

timnivas _____

droracbaytesh _____

Word Bank
proteins
vitamins
minerals
carbohydrates
water
fats

Nutrient Job Board
Match each nutrient from above with the job that it does for your body.

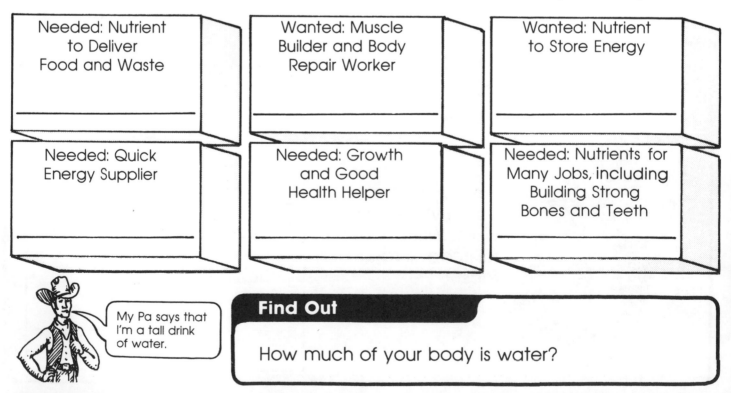

Needed: Nutrient to Deliver Food and Waste	Wanted: Muscle Builder and Body Repair Worker	Wanted: Nutrient to Store Energy
Needed: Quick Energy Supplier	Needed: Growth and Good Health Helper	Needed: Nutrients for Many Jobs, including Building Strong Bones and Teeth

My Pa says that I'm a tall drink of water.

Find Out

How much of your body is water?

The New "Big Four"

Name _____

Your body will get the nutrients it needs if you follow the rules of the food group pyramid. Be sure to make fruits, vegetables, and grains the basic foods of your diet. Eat plenty of healthy foods from the bottom of the pyramid every day.

oils, fats, sweets
eat very few

milk, yogurt, cheese –
2-3 servings daily

meat, fish, poultry, eggs, dry beans, nuts –
2-3 servings daily

fruits –
2-4 servings daily

vegetables –
3-5 servings daily

bread, cereal, pasta, rice –
6-11 servings each day

Find Out

What foods do you eat each day? Choose a day and make a chart of what you eat. Record the kind of food and the number of servings.

Group	Breakfast	Lunch	Dinner	Snack
Bread, cereal, pasta, rice				
Vegetables				
Fruits				
Meat, fish, poultry, eggs, dry beans, nuts				
milk, cheese, and yogurt				
Fats, oils, and sweets				

How did you do? Compare your servings with what is indicated on the food pyramid.

Go Power

Carbohydrates are the main source of quick energy. Foods with lots of sugar and starch are rich in carbohydrates. You get carbohydrates from many of your favorite foods like spaghetti, bread, cake, and candy.

Complete the sentences using words from the word bank.

Word Bank
fat
first
starches
energy

Carbohydrates are the _____ foods to be digested.

_____ are changed to sugars.

Sugar gives us _____.

Leftover sugar is stored as _____.

Fill in the plate with carbohydrate-rich foods. Find pictures of these foods in magazines, cut them out, and paste them on the plate.

Find Out

Sweet Test
1. Chew a soda cracker well. Keep it in your mouth for five minutes.
2. What is the new taste in your mouth?
3. What happened to the starch in the cracker?

Energy Savers

Name _____

Fats give you twice as much energy as protein or carbohydrates. Your body uses fats to save energy for future use. The fats we eat come from animals in the form of meat, eggs, milk, and much more. We also get fats from some plants like beans, peanuts, and corn. But not all plants give us fats in our diet.

Look at the pictures.
Circle the foods which are rich in fat.
Then list them on the chart.

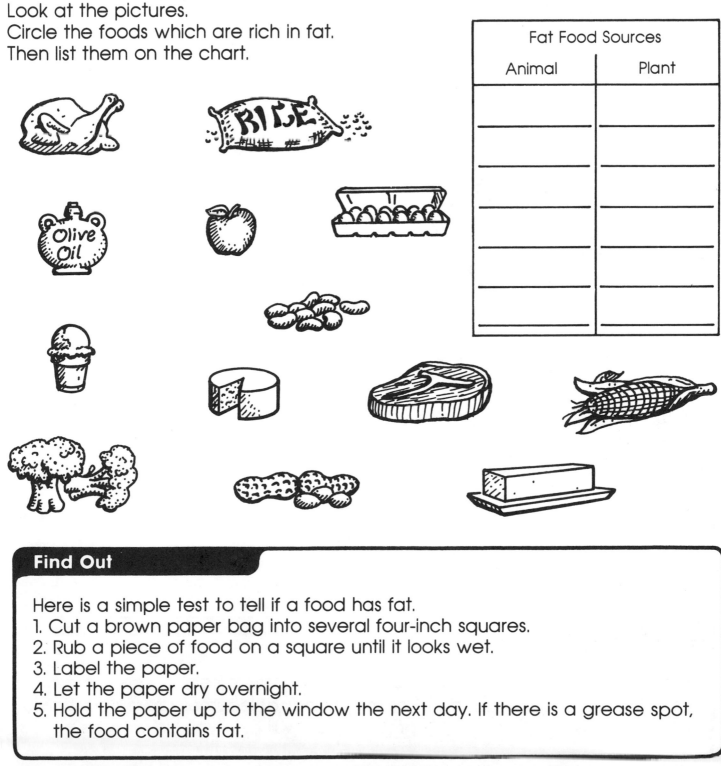

Fat Food Sources	
Animal	Plant

Find Out

Here is a simple test to tell if a food has fat.
1. Cut a brown paper bag into several four-inch squares.
2. Rub a piece of food on a square until it looks wet.
3. Label the paper.
4. Let the paper dry overnight.
5. Hold the paper up to the window the next day. If there is a grease spot, the food contains fat.

Protein:
The Body Builder

Name _____

Protein is the nutrient that repairs and builds new body tissue. Most of the foods we eat contain some protein. We call these "high protein foods."

Circle all of the high protein foods.

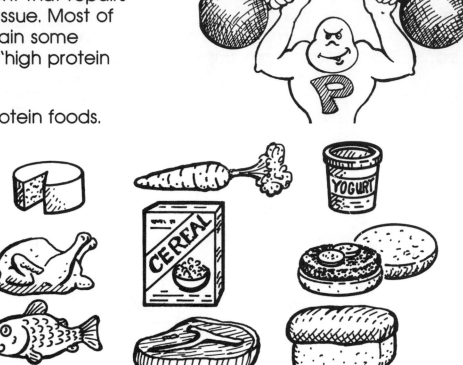

Did you notice that most of the foods you circled belong to two food groups? Name these groups and list the circled foods under the correct group. Add two more high protein foods to each list.

Group: _____   Group: _____

1. _____   1. _____

2. _____   2. _____

3. _____   3. _____

4. _____   4. _____

5. _____   5. _____

6. _____   6. _____

Find Out

Legumes (dry peas and beans) are an important protein source in many countries around the world. List as many kinds of legumes as you can think of. (Hint: A trip to your favorite grocery store will help you answer this.)

Amazing "Vita-Men"

Name _____

Vitamins do many important jobs. They help us grow and stay healthy. We can get all of the vitamins we need by eating a well-balanced diet.

Guide the Vita-Men through the mazes to find out the jobs they do.

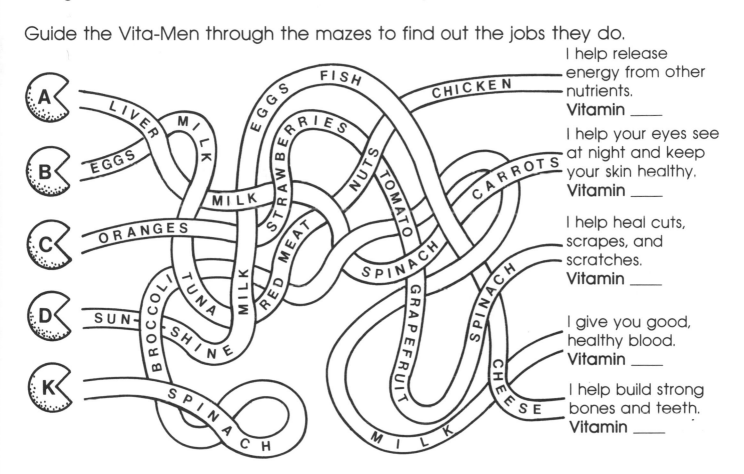

I help release energy from other nutrients.
Vitamin ____

I help your eyes see at night and keep your skin healthy.
Vitamin ____

I help heal cuts, scrapes, and scratches.
Vitamin ____

I give you good, healthy blood.
Vitamin ____

I help build strong bones and teeth.
Vitamin ____

List the food sources for each vitamin. (Hint: Use the maze.)

Vitamin A	Vitamin B	Vitamin C	Vitamin D	Vitamin K

Find Out

Sailors who were at sea for a long time often became sick with a disease called "scurvy." What is scurvy? Which one of the Vita-Men could help the sailors? Why were British sailors called "limies"?

Minerals

Name _____

Minerals like calcium and iron are very important nutrients. Calcium helps build strong bones and teeth. Iron helps build rich, healthy blood. Calcium and iron are found in many different kinds of food.

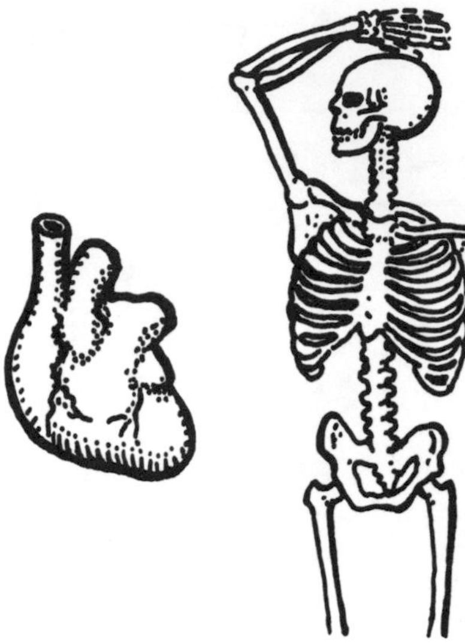

Circle the food words that are written across in the wordsearch. These foods are rich in iron. List them.

Circle the food words that are written up and down in the word search. These foods are rich in calcium. List them.

Iron-Rich Foods

_____
_____
_____
_____
_____

```
B A P B E A N S Y S
L B E F T M O K Y P
S R A I S I N S O C
G O N O Q L A P G H
R C U B F K Y I U E
U C T P E A S N R E
N O S N S B Z A T S
S L C L A M S C C E
L I V E R A H H Z B
```

Calcium-Rich Foods

_____
_____
_____
_____
_____

What calcium-rich or iron-rich foods have you eaten today? _____

_____

Find Out

Mystery Mineral: I am found in the toothpaste that you brush with each day. I am also added to water in some cities. I help fight tooth decay. What am I?

Tasty Plant Parts

Name _____

All of the fruits and vegetables you eat come from plant parts. Some parts are much tastier than others. Carrot roots probably tasto better than walnut tree roots.

Unscramble the names of the plant parts and label the pictures.

ealf _____   truif _____   frowel _____

smet _____   toors _____   eseds _____

Something Special

Garbage Gardening

1. Collect and wash the seeds from some fresh fruits and vegetables such as pumpkins, apples, or beans.
2. Soak the seeds overnight.
3. Plant the seeds ½ inch deep in a container of potting soil.
4. Keep the soil moist and in a warm place.
5. Watch for the seedlings!

©1992 Instructional Fair, Inc.   49   IF8758 Science Enrichment

Vegetable Stand

Name _____

Help Leon sort all of his produce.
List the letter of each of the fruits and vegetables under the correct plant part.

Fruity Vegetables   Circle the vegetables that are the fruits of the plant.

pea pod	cabbage	carrot	string bean
cucumber	avocado	broccoli	green pepper
spinach	zucchini	potato	turnip

Something Special

How many kinds of vegetables can you name? Write a list of as many vegetables as you can name. Circle the ones you like. Place an **X** in front of the ones you dislike. Place a **?** in front of the ones you have never tasted.

©1992 Instructional Fair, Inc.   IF8758 Science Enrichment

Pizza Party

Nutritious food is not dull, boring food. Angelo's pizza is very nutritious. It has food from all four food groups.

Match each ingredient with its food group.

Angelo's Pizza Supreme
1 loaf frozen bread dough, thawed
Mozzarella cheese (shredded)
hamburger (cooked)
pepperoni (sliced)
anchovies
sausage (cooked)
vegetable oil
pizza sauce (6 oz. can)
tomatoes (chopped)
onion (chopped)
green pepper (chopped)
mushrooms (sliced)
olives (sliced)

Bread and Cereal

Dairy

Meat and Protein

Fruit and Vegetable

Press thawed bread dough on pizza tin. Prick with a fork and brush with oil. Bake at 400° until light brown (about 10 minutes). Cover crust with tomato sauce, cheese, and other ingredients. Bake at 400° until cheese is melted.

Something Special

Have fun creating your own nutritious pizza recipe. You can use food from any of the four food groups. Share your recipe with your classmates. Which recipe sounds yummy? Which recipe sounds nutritious? Which recipe do you absolutely want to stay away from?

Labels

Name _____

Labels give us all kinds of information about the foods we eat. The ingredients of a food are listed in a special order. The ingredient with the largest amount is listed first, the one with the next largest amount is listed second, and so on.

Complete the "Breakfast Table Label Survey" using information from the label on this page.

Breakfast Table Label Survey

1. What does R.D.A. mean? _____

2. Calories per serving with milk _____

3. Calories per serving without milk _____

4. Calories per ½ cup serving of milk _____

5. Protein per serving with milk _____

6. Protein per serving without milk _____

7. Protein in ½ cup serving of milk _____

8. Percentage U.S. R.D.A. of Vitamin C _____

9. First ingredient _____

10. Is sugar a listed ingredient? _____

    If yes, in what place is it listed? _____

11. Were any vitamins added? _____

12. What preservative was added? _____

Find Out

What food product has this ingredient label? "Carbonated water, sugar, corn sweetener, natural flavorings, carmel color, phosphoric acid, caffeine."

Nutrition Information Per Serving

Serving Size: 1 OZ. (About 1⅓ Cups) (28.35 g)
Servings Per Package: 14

	1 OZ. (28.35 g) Cereal	with ½ Cup (118mL) Vitamin D Fortified Whole Milk
Calories	110	190
Protein	1 g	5 g
Carbohydrate	25 g	31 g
Fat	1 g	5 g
Sodium	195 mg	255 mg

Percentages Of U.S. Recommended Daily Allowances (U.S. RDA)

Protein	2%	8%
Vitamin A	25%	30%
Vitamin C	*	*
Thiamine	25%	30%
Riboflavin	25%	35%
Niacin	25%	25%
Calcium	*	15%
Iron	10%	10%
Vitamin D	10%	25%
Vitamin B_6	25%	30%
Folic Acid	25%	25%
Vitamin B_{12}	25%	30%
Phosphorus	2%	10%
Magnesium	2%	6%
Zinc	10%	15%
Copper	2%	4%

*Contains less than 2% of the U.S. RDA for these nutrients.

Ingredients: Corn Flour, Sugar, Oat Flour, Salt, Hydrogenated Coconut and/or Palm Kernel Oil, Corn Syrup, Honey and fortified with the following nutrients: Vitamin A Palmitate, Niacinamide, Iron, Zinc Oxide (Source of Zinc), Vitamin B_6, Riboflavin (Vitamin B_2), Thiamine Mononitrate (Vitamin B_1), Vitamin B_{12}, Folic Acid and Vitamin D_2. BHA added to packaging material to preserve freshness.

Carbohydrate Information

	1 OZ. (28.35 g) Cereal	With ½ Cup (118 mL) Whole Milk
Starch and Related Carbohydrates	14 g	14 g
Sucrose and Other Sugars	11 g	17 g
Total Carbohydrates	25 g	31 g

Munch, Munch – Nibble – Crunch!

Name _____

Do you have a bad case of the munchies, crunchies, or nibbles? Some snack foods can be good for you, while others are terrible. Foods that are lower on the food pyramid are usually much better for you because they contain smaller amounts of fat.

Take a **Snacker's Survey**.

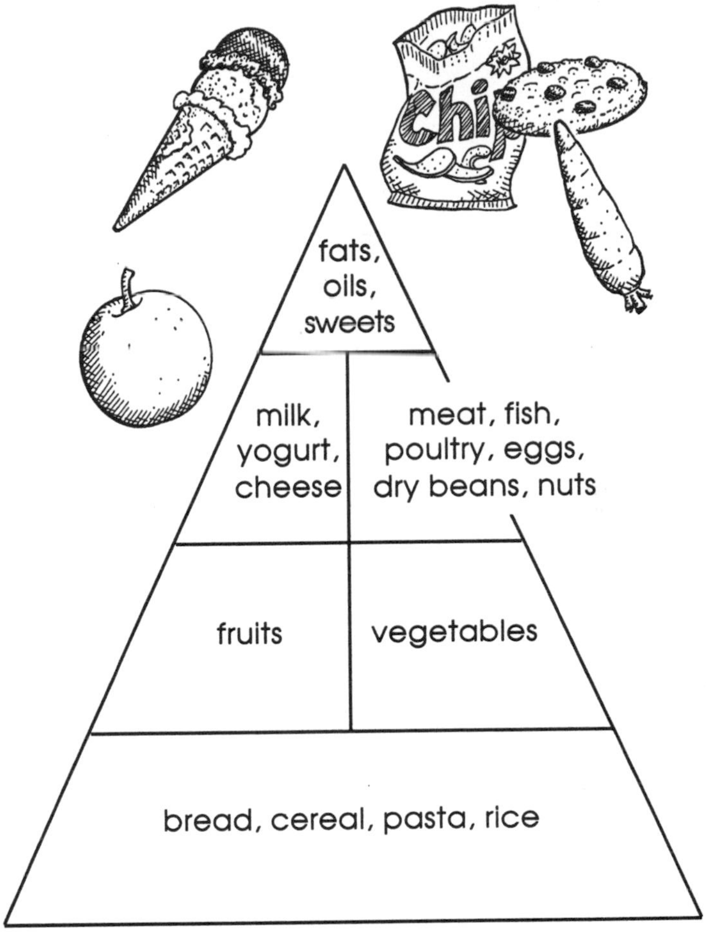

Snacker's Survey

Write the food group to which each snack belongs. Then, using a scale of 1-10, with 1 being the lowest, give each snack a taste score and a nutrition score.

Snack	Food Group	Taste Score	Nutrition Score
Apple			
Cheese			
Cookie			
Potato Chips			
Orange			
Carrot			
Cake			
Candy Bar			
Bagel			
Beef Jerky			
Popcorn			
Pretzels			

fats, oils, sweets

milk, yogurt, cheese

meat, fish, poultry, eggs, dry beans, nuts

fruits

vegetables

bread, cereal, pasta, rice

Fun Fact!

Labels might not use the name **sugar** when it lists a sweetener. Watch for other names for sugar.

Dextrose	Lactose
Corn Syrup	Fructose
Molasses	Sucrose

Push and Pull

Name _____

Look at the children in the picture. How are they moving their friends? A push or a pull on something is called a **force.** Forces can cause an object to move, slow down, speed up, change direction, or stop.

- You use pushing and pulling forces every day to move objects. List five ways that you use each of these forces.

Pushing Forces

1. _____
2. _____
3. _____
4. _____
5. _____

Pulling Forces

1. _____
2. _____
3. _____
4. _____
5. _____

- It takes more force to move some objects than it does to move others. Circle the object in each picture which would take more force to move.

Energy

Name _____

Do you feel tired after raking the lawn? You feel tired then because work takes a lot of energy. **Energy** is the ability to do work.

There are many forms of energy. Food contains **chemical energy.** Your television uses **electrical energy.** The furnace in your house gives you **heat energy.** The moving parts of your bicycle have another form of energy called **mechanical energy.** Anything that moves has mechanical energy.

Energy can be changed from one form to another. Your radio changes electrical energy into sound energy. Your parents' car may change chemical energy into heat energy, and the heat energy into mechancial energy.

• What kind of energy is being used to do work in each of these pictures?

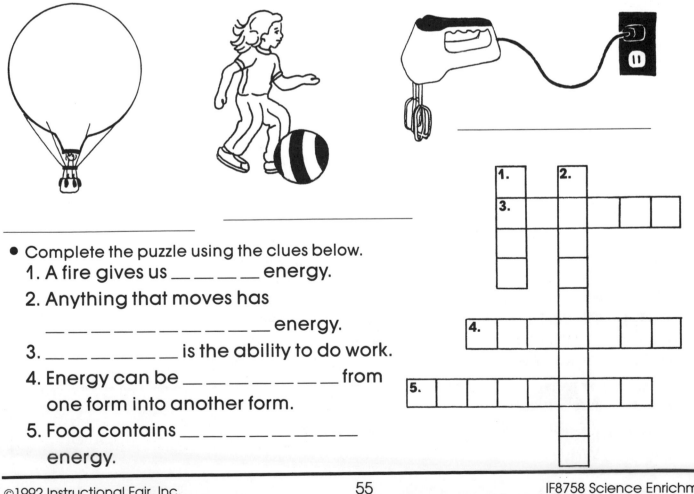

• Complete the puzzle using the clues below.
   1. A fire gives us __ __ __ __ energy.
   2. Anything that moves has
      __ __ __ __ __ __ __ __ __ __ energy.
   3. __ __ __ __ __ __ is the ability to do work.
   4. Energy can be __ __ __ __ __ __ __ __ from one form into another form.
   5. Food contains __ __ __ __ __ __ __ __ energy.

Energy in Motion

Name _____

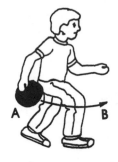

"Mom, how can I knock down more pins?" Matt asked. "You are bowling straight enough, Matt. Try rolling the ball faster, or try using a heavier ball," his mom replied.

The bowling ball is doing work by knocking over the pins. The ball has kinetic energy. **Kinetic energy** is the energy of motion.

If the ball had more kinetic energy, it could do more work and knock down more pins. If you increase the mass of the ball or its speed, you would increase its kinetic energy.

Just before Matt rolled the ball, he was standing still and not moving. Matt's body had stored energy that would turn into kinetic energy once he started swinging the ball. This stored energy is called **potential energy.**

• Write **P** next to the pictures that show potential energy and **K** next to the pictures that show kinetic energy.

• Look back at the picture of Matt getting ready to bowl.
   1. At what point will the ball have the most potential energy?_____
   2. At what point will the ball have the most kinetic energy?_____
   3. At what point will the ball have the least kinetic energy?_____
   4. At what point will the ball have the least potential energy?_____

Challenge

A roller-coaster car with more people in it will travel much faster than an empty car. Why?

Ramps, Hills, and Slopes

Name _____

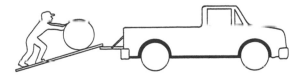

Word Bank

machine	easier
force	inclined
shorter	longer

- **Fill in the blanks with words from the Word Bank.**

     Simple machines help people do work. In the picture above, the ramp makes the man's work a lot _ _ _ _ _ _. The ramp is a simple _ _ _ _ _ _ _ called an inclined plane.

     An _ _ _ _ _ _ _ _ plane makes work easier. It lessens the amount of force needed to move a load. By using the ramp, the man moves the barrel with much less force than if he tried to lift the barrel himself. With the ramp, the man moves the barrel a _ _ _ _ _ _ distance, but with much less force. By just lifting the barrel onto the truck, he would move it a _ _ _ _ _ _ _ distance, but would need to use much more _ _ _ _ _.

- Ramps are used in many places to help people in wheelchairs get around more easily. List some places where ramps are used in your community.

     1. _____
     2. _____
     3. _____

     The angle of an inclined plane affects the amount of force needed to lift an object. The longer and less steep the inclined plane is, the less force it takes to lift an object.

- **Study the pictures below and then answer the questions.**

1. On which ramp will the barrel have to travel the farthest to get on the truck?_____
2. On which ramp will the least amount of force be needed to roll the barrel onto the truck?_____
3. How does the angle of the ramp affect the force needed to move the barrel?

_____

Find Out

How did the early Egyptians use inclined planes to build the great pyramids?

Special Inclined Planes

Name _____

"Poof!" Leroy just shrank himself again in his "Super Electro Shrinking Machine." He is trying to decide which would be easier–climbing around and around the threads of a screw to get to the top or just climbing straight up the side of the screw. He found that the distance up the winding ramp is a lot farther, but the traveling is much easier than going straight up the side. The winding ramp of the screw is like a spiral stairway.

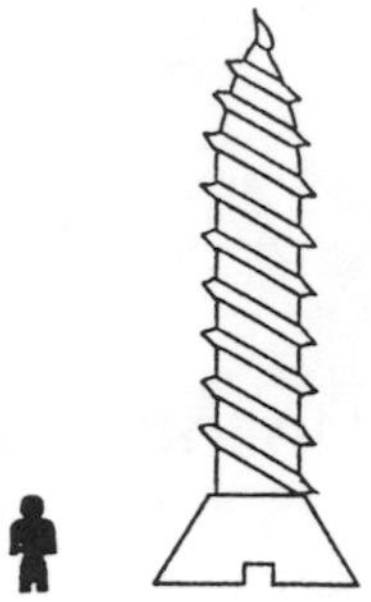

● **Answer these questions.**

1. Would you travel a farther distance climbing a spiral stairway up three floors or climbing a ladder straight up three floors?_____

2. Which would take more force to climb–the stairway or the ladder?_____

3. When you climb a spiral stairway, you travel a greater __ __ __ __ __ __ __ __, but you use less __ __ __ __ __.

A screw is a special kind of inclined plane. A spiral stairway is also an inclined plane.

Two or more inclined planes that are joined together to make a sharp edge or point form a wedge. A **wedge** is a special kind of inclined plane. A wedge is used to pierce or split things. A knife is a wedge. Can you name some other wedges?

● Some special inclined planes are pictured below. Label each picture either a wedge or a screw.

_____   _____   _____   _____

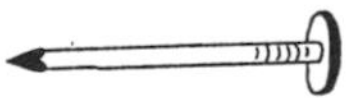

_____   _____

_____

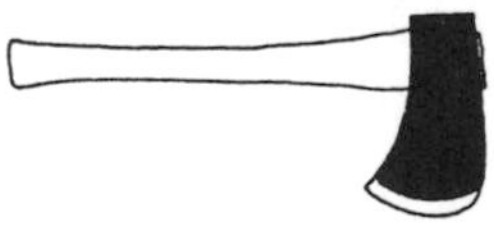

● Find these special inclined planes in the puzzle to the right.

nail	stairway
fork	screw
pin	axe
knife	wedge

```
W G T P I N O K
E X W B D Z K N
D A Z K F E N I
G S C R E W P F
E A S K A X E E
J R F T U N K L
P A T O N A I L
S T A I R W A Y
V R T N O K O T
```

_____

Levers

Name _____

Word Bank
simple   force
easier   load
fulcrum   distance
A   B

• Use the words from the Word Bank to complete the sentences.

    Mandy wants to try to lift her dad off the ground. Where should Mandy stand on the board? By standing on point __, Mandy can lift her dad.

    The board resting on the log is an example of a _ _ _ _ _ _ machine called a lever. A **lever** has three parts–the **force,** the **fulcrum,** and the **load.** Mandy is the force. The point on which the lever turns is called the _ _ _ _ _ _ _ _ . And Mandy's dad, the object to be lifted, is called the _ _ _ _ _. The greater the _ _ _ _ _ _ _ _ between the _ _ _ _ _ and the fulcrum, the _ _ _ _ _ _ it is to lift the load. The closer the distance between the **force** and the **fulcrum,** the harder it is to lift the load.

• Label the picture of Mandy and her father with these words: **load, force,** and **fulcrum.**

1

Fulcrum far away from load

2

Fulcrum close to load

    The distance between the **load** and the **fulcrum** also affects the force needed to lift a load. The closer the fulcrum is to the load, the easier it is to lift the load.

• Look at the pictures above to answer these questions.

  1. Matt wants to move a large rock with a lever. Which lever would let him use the least amount of force to move the rock?_____

  2. Which lever would have to be moved the greatest distance to move the rock?_____

  3. Why is a lever called a simple machine? _____

_____

• Label the **force, fulcrum,** and **load** of the levers below.

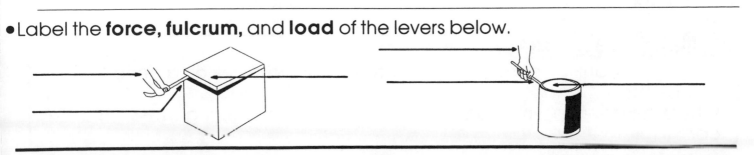

Around and Around

Name _____

A doorknob is a simple machine you use every day. It is a **wheel and axle machine.** The wheel is connected to the axle. The axle is a center post. When the wheel moves, the axle does too.

Opening a door by turning the axle with your fingers is very hard. But by turning the doorknob, which is the "wheel," you use much less force. The doorknob turns the axle for you. The doorknob makes it easy because it is much bigger than the axle. You turn the doorknob a greater distance, but with much less force.

Sometimes the "wheel" of a wheel and axle machine doesn't look like a wheel. But look at the path the doorknob, a wheel, makes when it is turned. The path makes a circle, just like a wheel.

• Color just the wheels of the wheel and axle machines below.

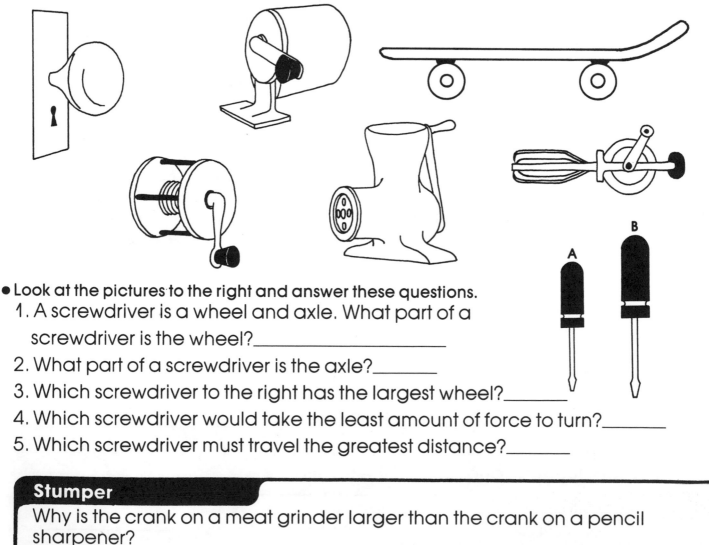

• Look at the pictures to the right and answer these questions.
  1. A screwdriver is a wheel and axle. What part of a screwdriver is the wheel?_____
  2. What part of a screwdriver is the axle?_____
  3. Which screwdriver to the right has the largest wheel?_____
  4. Which screwdriver would take the least amount of force to turn?_____
  5. Which screwdriver must travel the greatest distance?_____

Stumper

Why is the crank on a meat grinder larger than the crank on a pencil sharpener?

Why is the steering wheel on a truck larger than the steering wheel on a car?

Gearing Up

Name _____

An eggbeater has a special kind of wheel. It is called a gear. A **gear** is a wheel with teeth. The teeth allow one gear to turn another gear.

Gears are often used to increase or decrease speed. If the large gear in the picture turns one time, how many times will the small gear turn?

- Gears are found in many machines. Circle all of the machines you can find in the puzzle. Then list only the machines that use gears.

```
S T K N Z O R K G
H A M M E R U T K
O P S O R E R C N
V G Z V F A O T S
E B O I C L G X Z
L Z N E C B Z E K
D K X P W I Y G L
C K T R U C K G K
R R M O X Y T B G
A T N J S C U E H
K N R E R L V A Z
E G S C Q E W T R
P L K T G Z T E S
Z K P O H O X R T
Z U T R A M P N P
```

Machines with Gears

_____
_____
_____
_____
_____
_____

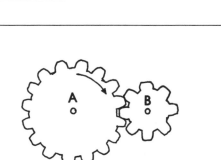

- Look at the picture to the right.

1. Draw an arrow on the picture showing the direction gear **B** will turn.

2. If gear **A** is turned one time, how many times will gear **B** turn?

Challenge

Look at the gears to the right. What will happen if gear **A** is turned?

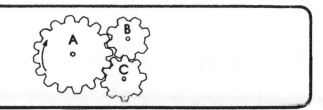

Work Savers

Name ______________________

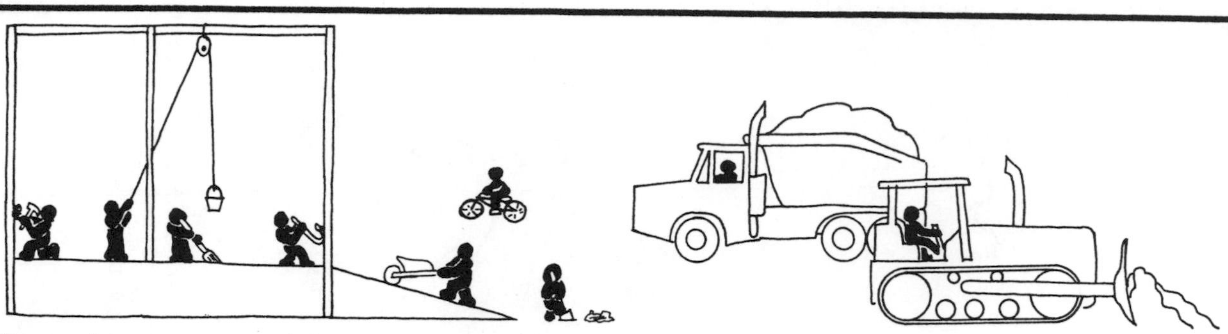

People use machines to help them with their work every day. Cars, trucks, sewing machines, and bicycles have many moving parts. They are called **compound machines.**

Some machines have few or no moving parts. They are called **simple machines.** A hammer, a pulley, and a ramp are all simple machines.

A simple machine makes work easier. It lets you do the work with less force, but you must pay something in return. You will have to move the object a greater distance.

- Look at the machines in the picture above. List each machine in the correct group.

Simple Machines

____

____

____

____

____

____

____

____

Compound Machines

____

____

____

____

- **Unscramble these mixed-up sentences.**

1. work machines make easier. ______________________

2. machines compound many have parts moving. ______________________

3. force machines less do with you let work. ______________________

4. machines no few or parts have moving simple. ______________________

©1992 Instructional Fair, Inc.

Simple + Simple = Compound

Name _____

gears

levers

wheel and axle machines

Many of the machines that you use each day are made up of two or more simple machines. What simple machines can you find in Mandy's bicycle? Find the gears, the wheel and axle machines, and the levers. Machines that are made up of two or more simple machines are called **compound machines.**

- Look carefully at the compound machines pictured on this page. Find the simple machines that make up each compound machine. Label the simple machines you find.

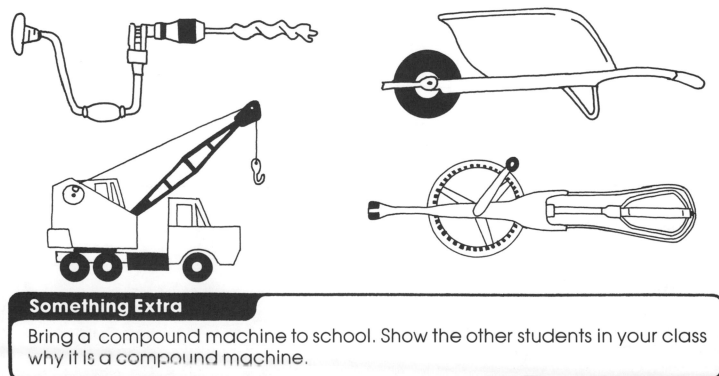

Something Extra

Bring a compound machine to school. Show the other students in your class why it is a compound machine.

Machines of Old

Name _____

Simple machines have been used for hundreds of years. The builders of the famous castles in Europe did not have modern machines. But they did have some simple machines to help them make their fabulous castles.

- Look carefully at the men building the castle. They are working hard, but their simple machines are missing. Draw in the missing machines. The Picture Bank at the bottom of the page will help you.

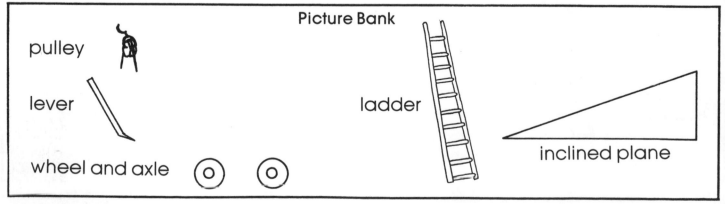

Picture Bank

pulley

lever

wheel and axle

ladder

inclined plane

©1992 Instructional Fair, Inc.   IF8758 Science Enrichment

Charge It!

Name _____

Have you ever scuffed your feet as you walked across the carpet and then brought your finger close to someone's nose? Zap!! Did the person jump? The spark you made was **static electricity.**

Static electricity is made when objects gain or lose tiny bits of electricity called **electrical charges.** The charges are either positive or negative.

Objects that have electrical charges act like magnets, attracting or repelling each other. If two objects have **like charges** (the same kind of charges), they will repel each other. If two objects have **unlike charges** (different charges), the objects will attract each other.

Find out more about static electricity by unscrambling the word(s) in each sentence.

1. Flashes of (ghtlining) _____ in the sky are caused by static electricity in the clouds.

2. Electrical charges are either (ospivite) _____ or (givnatee) _____.

3. Small units of electricity are called (srgache) _____.

4. Two objects with unlike charges will (arcttat) _____ each other.

5. Sometimes electric charges jump between objects with (unkile) _____ charges. This is what happens when lightning flashes in the sky.

Look at the pictures below to see how static electricity affects objects.

1. Name the two objects that are interacting in each picture.
2. Tell whether the two objects have **like charges** or **unlike charges.**

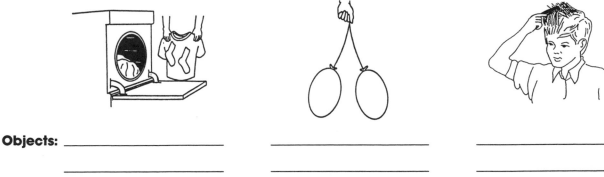

Objects: _____   _____   _____

_____   _____   _____

Charges: _____   _____   _____

Something Special

Hold this paper against a wall and rub it with 50 quick strokes with the side of your pencil. Take your hand away. Presto! The paper stays on the wall because of the static electricity you have made.

Power Paths

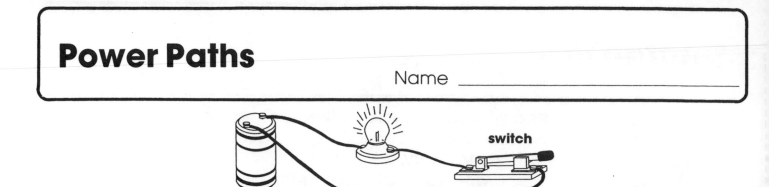

A **circuit** is a path along which electricity travels. It travels in a loop around the circuit. In the circuit pictured above, the electricity travels through the wire, battery, switch, and bulb. The electricity must have a source. What is the source in this circuit? You're right if you said the battery.

If the wire in the circuit was cut, there would be a **gap.** The electricity wouldn't be able to flow across the gap. Then the bulb would not light. This is an example of an **open circuit.** If there were no gaps, the bulb would light. This is an example of a **closed circuit.**

1. Draw in the wire to the battery, switch, and bulb to make a closed circuit.

 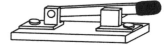

2. Draw in the wire to the battery, switch, and bulb to make an open circuit.

 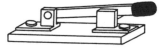

● Unscramble the word at the end of each sentence to fill in the blank.

3. Even the tiniest _____ can stop the electricity from flowing. (apg)

4. A _____ is a path along which electricity flows. (ricituc)

5. If there are no gaps, or openings, a _____ circuit is formed. (sodelc)

6. A battery is a source of _____ in some circuits. (treleciytci)

Fun Fact

If all of the circuits in a small personal computer were made out of wire and metal switches, the computer would fill the average classroom. Today these circuits are found in tiny chips called microchips.

Fill the Gap

Name _____

The bulb won't light in the circuit above. What's wrong with the circuit? It has a gap. How could you fill the gap to make a closed circuit? The easiest way would be to connect the two wires, but with what?

What would happen if you placed a paper clip across the gap? How about a nail? The bulb would light up. The nail or paper clip would form a bridge across the gap. The nail and paper clip carry, or **conduct,** electricity. They are both **conductors.**

Some materials will not carry the electricity well enough to make the bulb light. Try a rubber band. The bulb won't light. Rubber is a poor conductor of electricity. It is called an **insulator.**

• Find the different materials hidden in the wordsearch. The materials listed "up and down" are conductors. Those written "across" are insulators. List these materials in the correct group.

```
C O T T O N P
O K G T S O R
P A P E R X K
P L A S T I C
E U D T O R D
R M K E L O S
T I X E R N N
N N G L A S S
R U B B E R Z
K M G R X Z P
```

Insulator

_____

_____

_____

_____

_____

Conductor

_____

_____

_____

_____

• Now that you know which materials make good conductors and which make good insulators, write **C** under each object that is a conductor and **I** under each object that is an insulator.

Name _____

In 1877, Samuel Morse used electricity to make the first telegraph. This invention allowed people to communicate directly with one another over long distances.

Study the picture of the simple telegraph. Notice how the switch, light bulb, battery, and wire form a circuit. Use the symbols in the key to draw a diagram of the telegraph.

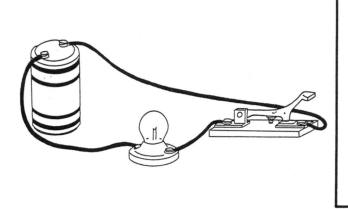

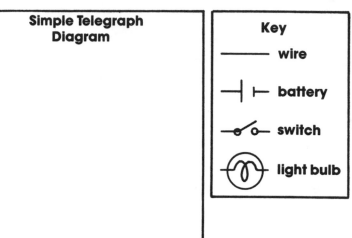

Simple Telegraph Diagram

Key
——— wire
—┤ ├— battery
—•⌒•— switch
—(⊕)— light bulb

Morse Code

				U ••—
A •—	F ••—•	K —•—	P •——•	V •••—
B —•••	G ——•	L •—••	Q ——•—	W •——
C —•—•	H ••••	M ——	R •—•	X —••—
D —••	I ••	N —•	S •••	Y —•——
E •	J •———	O ———	T —	Z ——••

Decode the following message.

•—— •—• •• — •   •—   ••• • —•—• •—• • —

—— •• ••• ••• •— —••—• •   — ———   •—

••—• •—• •• • —• —••

Find Out

In 1876, Alexander Graham Bell used his new invention, the telephone, to make the first telephone call. He said, "Mr. _____, come here, I want to see you." To find the name of the first person to receive a telephone call, decode the title of this page.

Series or Parallel?

Name _____

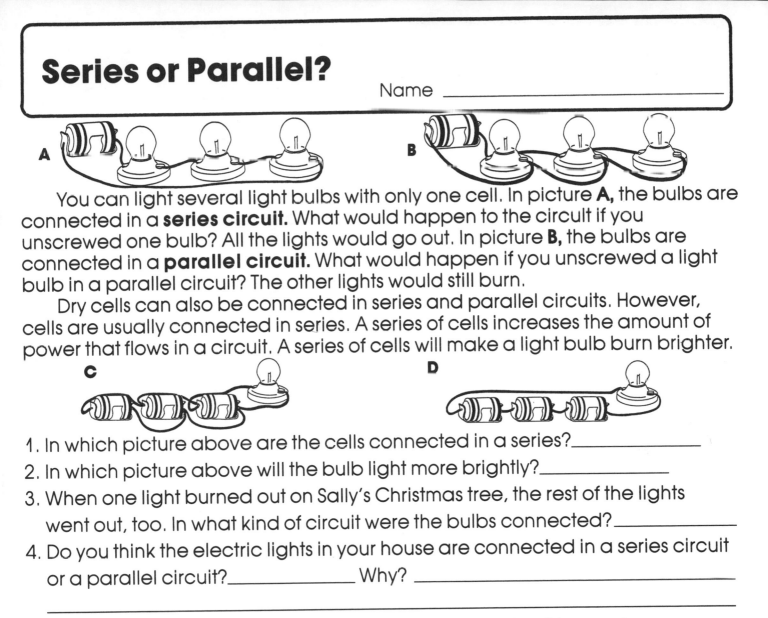

You can light several light bulbs with only one cell. In picture **A,** the bulbs are connected in a **series circuit.** What would happen to the circuit if you unscrewed one bulb? All the lights would go out. In picture **B,** the bulbs are connected in a **parallel circuit.** What would happen if you unscrewed a light bulb in a parallel circuit? The other lights would still burn.

Dry cells can also be connected in series and parallel circuits. However, cells are usually connected in series. A series of cells increases the amount of power that flows in a circuit. A series of cells will make a light bulb burn brighter.

1. In which picture above are the cells connected in a series?_____

2. In which picture above will the bulb light more brightly?_____

3. When one light burned out on Sally's Christmas tree, the rest of the lights went out, too. In what kind of circuit were the bulbs connected?_____

4. Do you think the electric lights in your house are connected in a series circuit or a parallel circuit?_____ Why? _____

_____

5. How are the batteries connected in the flashlight below? In a series or parallel?_____

6. Some flashlights have four or five cells. How would the brightness of the light from this kind of flashlight compare with one that only has one or two cells?

_____

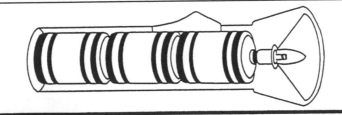

Fun Fact

A single dry cell is often called a battery, but it really isn't a battery. A battery is two or more cells connected together. You can buy batteries that look like a single cell, but they are really two or more cells connected together and put inside one case.

Light Up Your Life

Name _____

A light bulb changes electricity into light. Electricity passes through the very thin wire, called a **filament**, inside the bulb. As electricity flows through the filament, the wire gets hot and gives off light.

Look very closely at the filament in a light bulb. It is made of tiny coils of wire. By using coils, more wire can be put in the bulb—so more light can be made.

• Label the parts of the light bulb using the descriptions from the Word Bank.

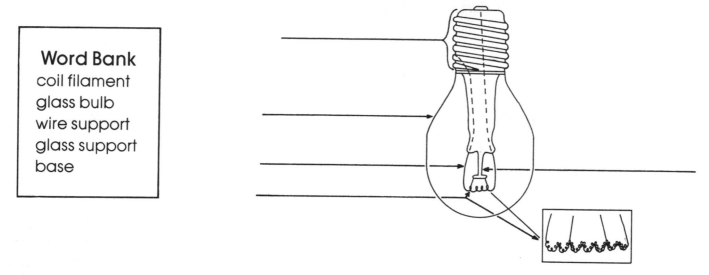

Word Bank
coil filament
glass bulb
wire support
glass support
base

On the top of a light bulb, you will see numbers and letters, such as **60W** or **100W,** or 60 watts and 100 watts. This tells you how much power the bulb uses. The more power the bulb uses, the brighter it glows.

1. Which light bulb uses the most electricity?_____

2. Which light bulb would make a good night light in your bedroom?_____

3. Which light bulb would glow the brightest?_____

4. Which light bulb would be a good light for reading?_____

Find Out

The first light bulb ever made had a filament made out of cotton! It burned brightly, but didn't last long. Find out who invented the first light bulb and when it was invented.

Making Electricity

Name _____

Where does the electricity that is in your house come from? It all begins at a large **power plant.** The power plant has a large **turbine generator.** High pressure steam spins the turbines and the generator that Is attached to the turbine shaft. As the generator spins, it produces hundreds of megawatts of electricity.

• Below is a picture of a power plant where electricity is generated. Label each part using the terms found in the Power Bank below.

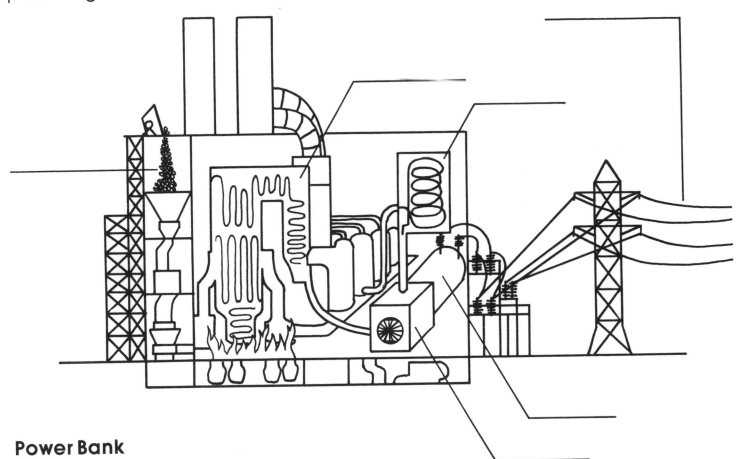

Power Bank

FUEL – Fuel, such as coal, enters the power plant.

BOILER – The burning fuel heats water in the boiler, making high pressure steam.

TURBINE – High pressure steam spins the blades of the turbine up to 3,000 times a minute.

CONDENSER – Steam is cooled in the condenser and is turned back into water. The water is sent back to the boiler.

GENERATOR – The generator attached to the turbine turns, producing hundreds of megawatts of electricity.

POWER LINES – Electricity is sent to your home through wires.

Portable Power

Name _____

Steve and Lenny really enjoyed listening to the radio while they fished. Radios need electricity to work. Where did Steve's radio get its power? From a **dry cell battery,** of course. Dry cells are sources of portable power.

Most portable radios use dry cells. A dry cell makes electricity by changing chemical energy into electrical energy. Chemicals in the dry cell act on each other and make **electrons** flow. The flow of electrons is called **electricity.**

● Use the words from the Word Bank to label the parts of the dry cell. You can use your science book to help, but first try to figure out each part by yourself.

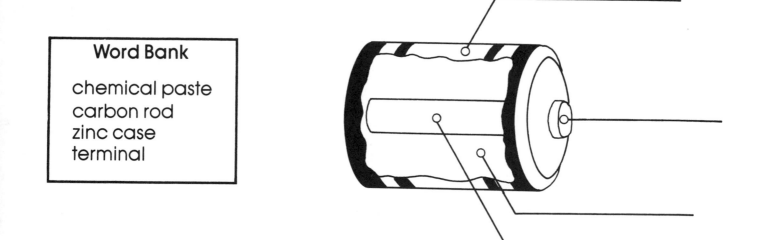

Word Bank

chemical paste
carbon rod
zinc case
terminal

Portable Power Inventory

List the appliances, tools, or toys in your house that are powered with dry cells.

_____   _____
_____   _____
_____   _____
_____   _____
_____   _____

Find Out

Before batteries were invented, scientists did all their experiments with static electricity. Find out who made the first battery and when it was made.

Conserving Electricity

Name _____

"Jane, did you remember to turn off the TV?" Jane's parents want Jane to remember to conserve electricity. It takes a lot of fuel to make electricity. We have to be careful not to waste electricity.

Your house has an **electric meter** that measures the amount of electricity your family uses. The meter measures the electricity in **kilowatt hours.** It would take one kilowatt hour to light ten light bulbs (100 watts each) for one hour. Would a 75 watt light bulb use more or less power than the 100 watt light bulb?

Look carefully at Jane in her home. How could Jane conserve electricity?

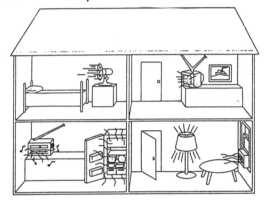

1. _____
2. _____
3. _____
4. _____
5. _____
6. _____

The electric meter on Jane's house is shown in Picture **A** below. It reads 2,563 kilowatt hours. Picture **B** shows Jane's electric meter after one month. Write the number of kilowatt hours shown on the meter. Then figure out the number of kilowatt hours Jane's family used in one month.

A.

2 5 6 3 kilowatts

B.

_ _ _ _ kilowatts

$$\begin{array}{r} \_\ \_\ \_\ \_ \\ -\ 2\ 5\ 6\ 3 \\ \hline \_\ \_\ \_\ \_ \end{array}$$

kilowatt hours

Find Out

Read your electric meter at home. Have your mother or father help you. Record the number of kilowatts. Read your meter one day later. Find out how much electricity your family has used. Keep a record every day for one week. What days did you use the most electricity?

The Invisible Force

Name _____

Hold a magnet close to a piece of metal. Do you feel a strange pulling force? Magnets are attracted to certain metals. The invisible force is called **magnetism.**

What kinds of objects will a magnet pull? The best and the most fun way to find out is to experiment. Gather some of the objects listed below. Hold a small magnet next to these objects. Which objects will the magnet pull? Add some of your own objects to the list.

Object	Magnet Attracts	Magnet Does Not Attract
scissors		
wood ruler		
eraser		
paper clip		
thumbtack		
paper		
aluminum foil		

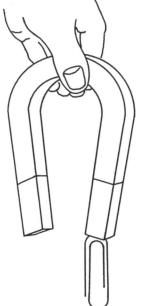

Magnets do not attract all metals. Find the six metals in the wordsearch. The metals that are written "up and down" are attracted to magnets. The metals written "across" are not attracted. List each metal in the correct group.

```
B N B R A S S X
Z I K L N T I A
A C O P P E R D
N K T R O E O S
T E K G N L N P
A L U M I N U M
```

Attracted
By
Magnets

_____

_____

_____

Not
Attracted
By
Magnets

_____

_____

_____

Fantastic Fact

Magnets were named after a shepherd called Magnes. A legend says that magnets were first discovered when Magnes stood on a rock. His sandals stuck to the rock when the nails in the sandals stuck to the "magic" rock. The magic rock was lodestone, a natural form of a magnet.

Push and Pull

Name _____

The ends of a magnet are called its **poles.** One pole is called the north-seeking pole, or **north pole.** The other is the south-seeking pole, or **south pole.**

When the poles of two bar magnets are put near each other, they have a force that will either pull them together or push them apart. If the poles are **different,** then they will pull together, or **attract** each other. (One pole is a south pole and one pole is a north pole.) If the poles are the **same,** then they will push apart, or **repel** each other. (They are either both south poles or both north poles.) The push and pull force of a magnet is called **magnetism.**

1. If these magnets are brought toward each other, will they **attract** or **repel** each other?

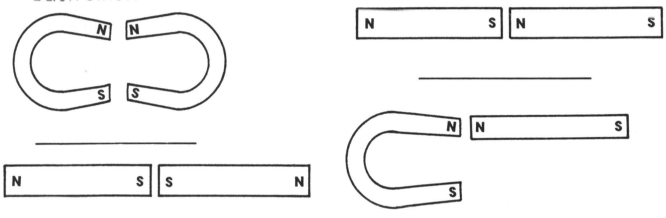

2. Look at each picture. Does the **?** show a north pole or a south pole?

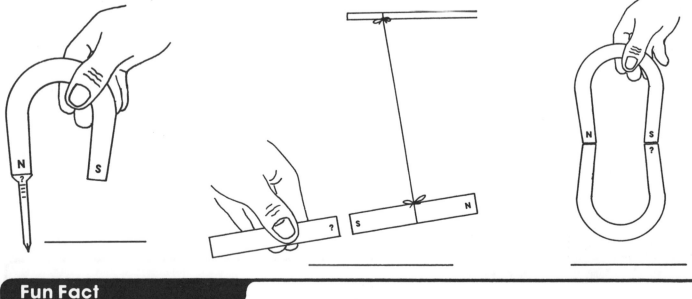

Fun Fact

If a magnet is broken into pieces, each piece will have a north pole and a south pole.

The North Pole

Name _____

The earth is like a big magnet. The earth has magnetic poles just like a magnet. The earth's magnetic poles are near the earth's **true poles.**

A **compass** is a free turning magnet. Compasses that you buy are made with a thin magnet, called a **needle,** that turns freely inside a case. The case is made of a nonmagnetic material. The north-seeking pole of the magnet is attracted toward the earth's **magnetic north pole.** The other end points to the **magnetic south pole.** A compass helps you find the directions north and south.

There is a **compass rose** in the corner of Elgin's map. The compass rose gives the eight compass directions: North (N), South (S), East (E), West (W), Northeast (NE), Southeast (SE), Southwest (SW), and Northwest (NW).
- Use the direction abbreviations to complete the compass rose on Elgin's map.
- Follow the directions to find where the secret treasure is buried. Each box is equal to one step.

Directions

1. Start at the star.
2. Go North 5 steps.
3. Go East 9 steps.
4. Go Southwest 4 steps.
5. Go East 2 steps.
6. Go South 2 steps.
7. Go Northeast 4 steps.
8. Dig here. You have reached the secret treasure.

Note:

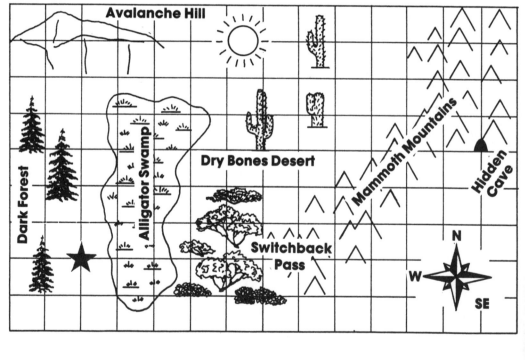

Stumper

While leaning against his dad's car, Elgin noticed that his compass would not point to north. What was the problem?

Magnet Magic

Name _____

It is a lot of fun to play with magnets. In the pictures below are some "tricks" that you can do to amaze your friends. Under each picture, explain why each of these amazing things happens.

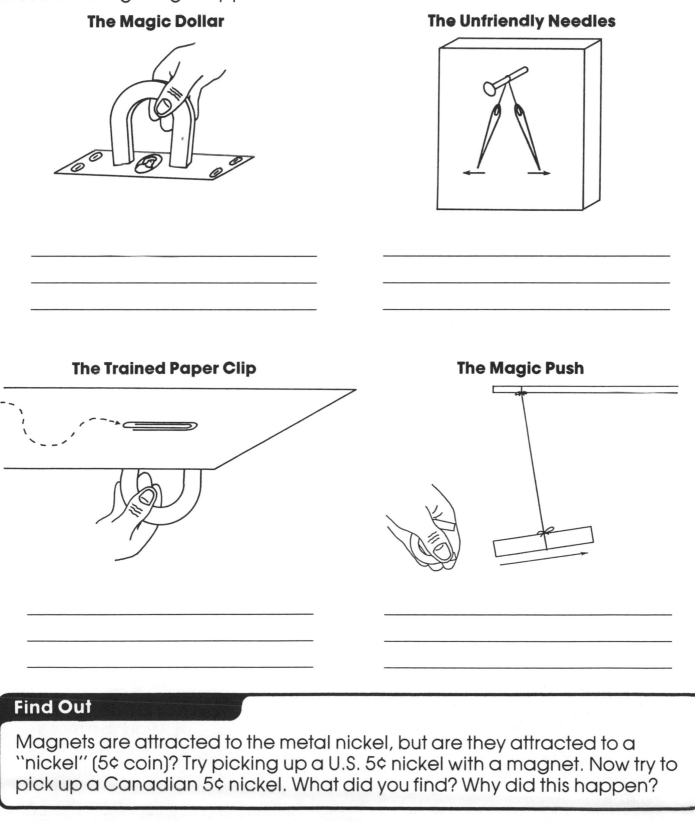

The Magic Dollar

_____
_____
_____

The Unfriendly Needles

_____
_____
_____

The Trained Paper Clip

_____
_____
_____

The Magic Push

_____
_____
_____

Find Out

Magnets are attracted to the metal nickel, but are they attracted to a "nickel" (5¢ coin)? Try picking up a U.S. 5¢ nickel with a magnet. Now try to pick up a Canadian 5¢ nickel. What did you find? Why did this happen?

Electromagnets

Name _____

Some of the most powerful magnets are made with electricity. These magnets are called **electromagnets.** A strong magnet can be made by winding wire around an iron bar. As soon as the current from a battery is switched on, the bar becomes a strong electromagnet. The magnet can be switched off by stopping the flow of current.

Larry and Eddie each made an electromagnet. Only one of them worked.

1. Whose electromagnet worked? _____
2. Why wouldn't the other electromagnet work? _____
   _____

3. Electromagnets have many uses and can be found in many places. Circle and list the objects in the wordsearch which use electromagnets.

1. _____
2. _____
3. _____
4. _____
5. _____
6. _____
7. _____
8. _____

```
T D O O R B E L L T
E T A B E K J S R A
L X O L F V R E L P
E S T E R E O T R E
V A E L I T H O N R
I M L O G U A R B E
S P E R E N O G L C
I X P L R K A M I O
O R H R A D I O T R
N R O L T U P R O D
B A N M O T O R K E
S H E L R M U S L R
```

Find Out

Make an electromagnet like the one in the picture above.
1. What happens to the strength of your electromagnet if you use more turns of wire?
2. Is your electromagnet still magnetic when you disconnect it from the battery?

Spinning Top

Name _____

Whir-r-r-ling! Matt's top is spinning very fast. Just like Matt's top, the Earth is also spinning.

The Earth spins about an imaginary line that is drawn from the North Pole to the South **Pole** through the center of the Earth. This line is called Earth's **axis.** Instead of using the word "spin," though, we say that the Earth **rotates** on its axis.

The Earth rotates **one** time every 24 hours. The part of the Earth facing the sun experiences day. The side that is away from the sun's light experiences **night.**

Draw a line from each picture of Matt to the correct day or night picture of the Earth.

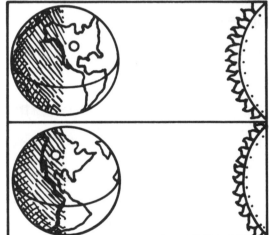

Use the words in bold above to solve the puzzle.

1. The part of the Earth not facing the sun experiences _____.
2. Earth's axis goes from the North to the South _____.
3. The Earth spins.
4. Number of times the Earth rotates in 24 hours.
5. Imaginary line on which the Earth rotates.

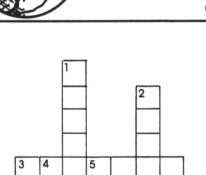

Fun Fact

At the Equator, the Earth is spinning at a speed of almost 1,600 km per hour. At a point halfway between the poles and the Equator, the speed is 1,300 km per hour. Spin a globe and you will see how this happens.

Lo-o-o-ong Trip

Name _____

What is the longest trip you have ever taken? Was it 100 km? 500 km? Maybe it was more than 1,000 km. You probably didn't know it, but last year you traveled 1 billion kilometers.

The Earth travels in a path around the sun called its **orbit.** Earth's orbit is almost 1 billion kilometers. It takes 1 year, or 365 days, for the Earth to orbit or **revolve** around the sun.

Look at the picture of Earth's orbit.
It is not a perfect circle.
It is a special shape called an **ellipse.**

1. How long does it take for the Earth to revolve around the sun? _____

2. How many times has the Earth revolved around the sun since you were born?

_____

3. How many kilometers has the Earth traveled in orbit since you were born?

_____

4. Put an "X" on Earth's orbit to show where it will be in six months.

Experiment

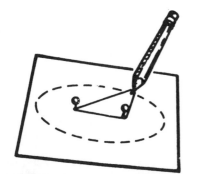

You can draw an ellipse. Place two straight pins about 8 cm apart in a piece of cardboard. Tie the ends of a 25 cm piece of string to the pins. Place your pencil inside the string. Keeping the string tight, draw an ellipse.

Make four different ellipses by changing the length of the string and the distance between the pins. How do the ellipses change?

Fun Fact

Hold on tight. The Earth travels at a speed of 100,000 km per hour in its orbital path around the sun.

Leaning Into Summer

Why isn't it summer all year long? The seasons change because the Earth is tilted like the leaning Tower of Pisa. As the Earth orbits the sun, it stays tilting in the same direction in space.

Let's look at the seasons in the Northern Hemisphere. When the North Pole is tilting toward the sun, the days become warmer and longer. It is summer. Six months later, the North Pole tilts away from the sun. The days become cooler and shorter. It is winter.

Label the Northern Hemisphere's seasons on the chart below. Write a make-believe weather forecast for each season. Each forecast should show what the weather is like in your region for that season.

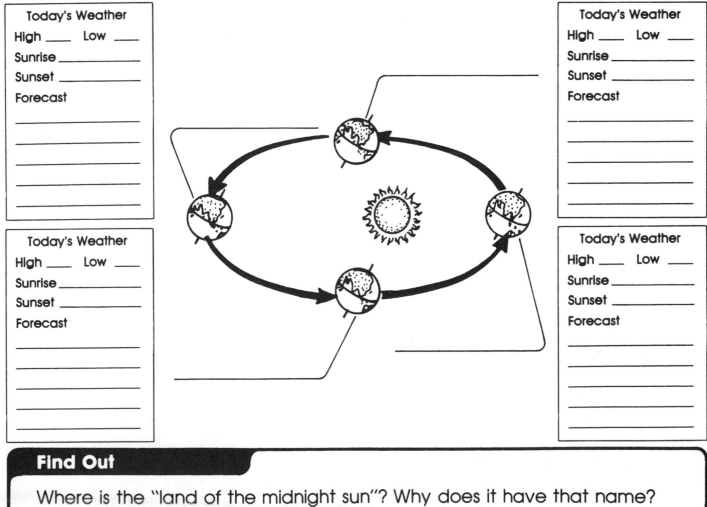

Today's Weather

High ____ Low ____

Sunrise _____

Sunset _____

Forecast

_____
_____
_____
_____
_____

Today's Weather

High ____ Low ____

Sunrise _____

Sunset _____

Forecast

_____
_____
_____
_____
_____

Today's Weather

High ____ Low ____

Sunrise _____

Sunset _____

Forecast

_____
_____
_____
_____
_____

Today's Weather

High ____ Low ____

Sunrise _____

Sunset _____

Forecast

_____
_____
_____
_____
_____

Find Out

Where is the "land of the midnight sun"? Why does it have that name?

Moon's "Faces"

Name _____

As the moon orbits the Earth, we often see different amounts of the moon's lighted part. Sometimes it looks like a circle, half-circle, or thin, curved sliver. These different shapes are the moon's **phases.**

Cut out the moon's phases as seen from Earth at the bottom of the page. Paste them next to the moon phase as seen from space. Label the pictures using the words in the word bank. Use your science book to help you.

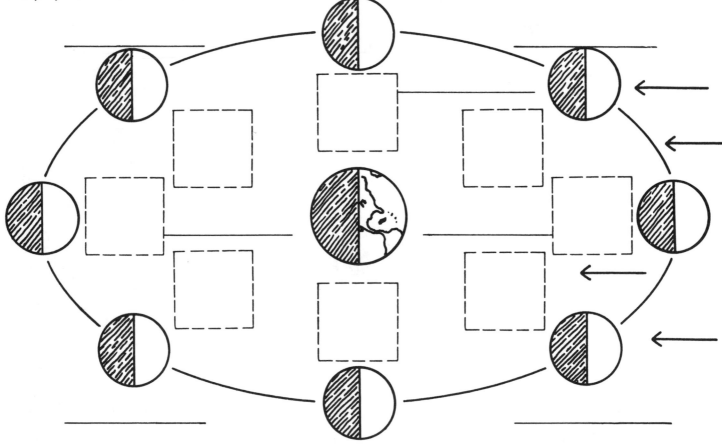

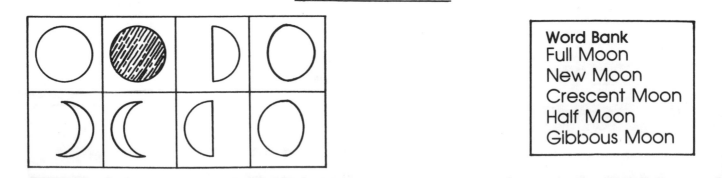

Word Bank
Full Moon
New Moon
Crescent Moon
Half Moon
Gibbous Moon

Space Shadows

Have you ever held your hand up in front of a bright light to make shadow pictures on the wall? The sun and moon can cast shadows on the Earth just like the light and your hand cast shadow pictures on the wall.

Sometimes the moon passes between the Earth and the sun in just the right place to cast a shadow on the Earth. It's a little eerie if you live in the place where the shadow falls. The sky darkens. The air becomes cooler. It seems like the middle of the night. This is called a **solar eclipse.**

Write "solar eclipse" on the picture which best shows one.

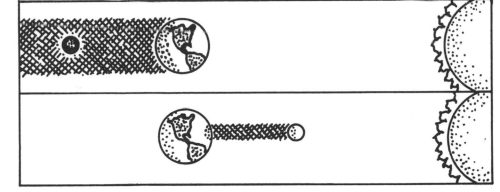

The moon casts an eerie shadow on the Earth during a solar eclipse. Ordinary objects can also cast eerie shadows when the light hits them at different angles. Circle the object that formed the shadow.

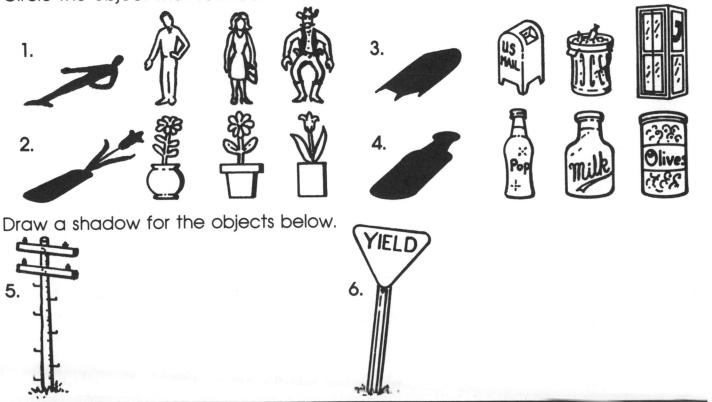

Draw a shadow for the objects below.

5.

6.

Wandering Stars

Name _____

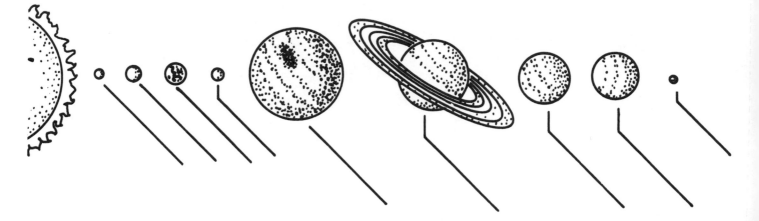

Many years ago the early astronomers noticed that a few "stars" seemed to roam about in the night sky. They named these stars **planets,** which means "wanderers."

We know that the planets are not stars. Stars make their own light, while planets shine by **reflecting** the sun's light. Planets don't wander in the sky either. Each planet revolves around the sun in its own path, or **orbit.**

Use the chart to label each planet above.

Planet	Distance from The Sun	Size (Diameter)
Mercury	58,000,000 km	4,880 km
Venus	108,000,000 km	12,100 km
Earth	150,000,000 km	12,756 km
Mars	228,000,000 km	6,794 km
Jupiter	778,000,000 km	143,200 km
Saturn	1,425,000,000 km	120,000 km
Uranus	2,867,000,000 km	51,800 km
Neptune	4,486,000,000 km	49,500 km
Pluto	5,890,000,000 km	2,600 km

Complete the puzzle using clues from the chart.
1. Planet almost the same size as Earth
2. Closest planet to the Sun
3. Largest planet
4. The smallest planet

Something Special

You can use the playground to make a model of the distances of each planet from the sun. One person will be the sun. Have the others take the following number of steps to show the distance from the sun. Mercury 1, Venus 2, Earth 3, Mars 4, Jupiter 13, Saturn 24, Uranus 48, Neptune 75, Pluto 98.

Planet Match

Name _____

Game Card

Mercury	Venus	Earth
Mars	Jupiter	Saturn
Uranus	Neptune	Pluto

1. Study the fact cards for each planet.
2. Cut out the cards and place them upside down on your desk.
3. You and your partner should each have a game card.
4. Take turns with your partner flipping over one card and matching it with the correct planet on your game card.
5. The first person to get 3 in a row, up and down, across, or diagonally is the winner.
6. Use your science book to make additional cards.

Mercury	Closest planet to the sun	This planet orbits the sun in the fewest days–88.
Venus	Known as "Earth's Sister"	Earth's nearest planet neighbor
Earth	The only planet with life	Known as the "Blue Planet"
Mars	"The Red Planet"	Orbits the sun between Earth and Jupiter

Jupiter	Largest planet	Has a "red spot" caused by windstorms
Saturn	Known for its beautiful rings	Second largest planet
Uranus	This planet spins on its side.	Orbits between Saturn and Neptune
Neptune	Most distant of the "giant planets"	Orbits between Uranus and Pluto
Pluto	Smallest planet	Has the farthest orbit from the sun

Space Snowballs

Name _____

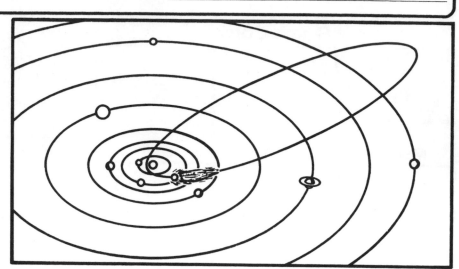

Planets and moons are not the only objects in our solar system that travel in orbits. Comets also orbit the sun.

A **comet** is like a giant dirty snowball from 1 to 5 kilometers wide. It is made of frozen gases, dust, ice, and rocks.

As the comet gets closer to the sun, the frozen gases melt and evaporate. Dust particles float in the air. The dust forms a cloud called a **coma.** The "wind" from the sun blows the coma away from the sun. The blowing coma forms the comet's tail.

There are more than 800 known comets. Halley's Comet is the most famous. It appears about every 76 years. 1985 is the last scheduled appearance in this century. When will it appear next?

Find the words from the word bank in the wordsearch. When you are finished, write down the letters that are not circled. Start at the top of the puzzle and go from left to right.

Word Bank	
dust	orbit
Halley	tail
coma	ice
snowball	sky
melt	shining
solar system	

```
S P M E L T L A N H E
O T S S H A C O M A V
L E N O R D B I T L S
A L O I K U E C I L R
R C W L E S S C O E M
S E B T S T H A V Y E
Y O A R O R B I T B I
S T L S S H A P E D L
T I L K T A I L E A F
E O O T I C E B A L L
M S K Y S H I N I N G
```

_ _ _ _ _ _ _ _ _ _ _ _ _ _ _ _ _ _   _ _ _ _

_ _ _ _ _ _ _ .   _ _ _ _ _ _ _ _ _ _   _ _ _ _ _ _

_ _ _ _ _ _ _   _ _ _ _ _ _   _   _ _ _ _ _ _ _ _ .

Star Light, Star Bright

Name _____

Lay on your back. Gaze up into the night sky. Which star is the brightest? On a clear night you can see hundreds of stars–some are bright and others are dim.

Why are some stars brighter than others? Let's try to find out by looking at the picture on this page.

1. Look at the two street lights in the picture. Which street light appears

   the brightest? _____

   Why? _____

   _____

2. Look at the bicycle and the truck. Which headlights appear the brightest? _____

   Why? _____

3. Some stars appear brighter than other stars for the same reasons as the lights in the picture. What are the two reasons.

   a. _____

   b. _____

Color Me Hot

Stars differ not only in brightness, but they also differ in color. As a star gets hotter, the color changes.
Color these stars. Use the chart to find the correct color.

Star Color	
Temperature	Color
20,000° C	Blue
10,000° C	White
5,000° C	Yellow
3,000° C	Red

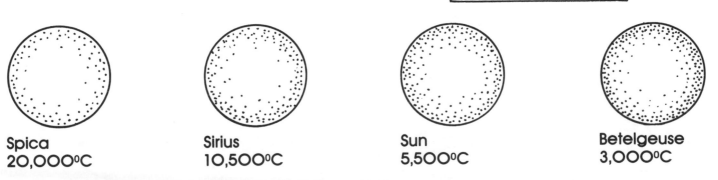

Spica
20,000°C

Sirius
10,500°C

Sun
5,500°C

Betelgeuse
3,000°C

Pictures in the Sky

Name _____

On a clear night, you can see hundreds of stars. You can probably see the Big Dipper or the Little Dipper. Try to make other pictures among the stars. Can you see animals or people?

Long ago, people spent hours gazing at the stars. They named groups of stars that formed pictures. We call these pictures **constellations.**

Color and cut out the constellations on this page. Make a mobile as pictured. Use your science book or other books to make pictures of other constellations for your mobile.

Cover a hanger with black paper and punch in holes to show some of your favorite constellations.

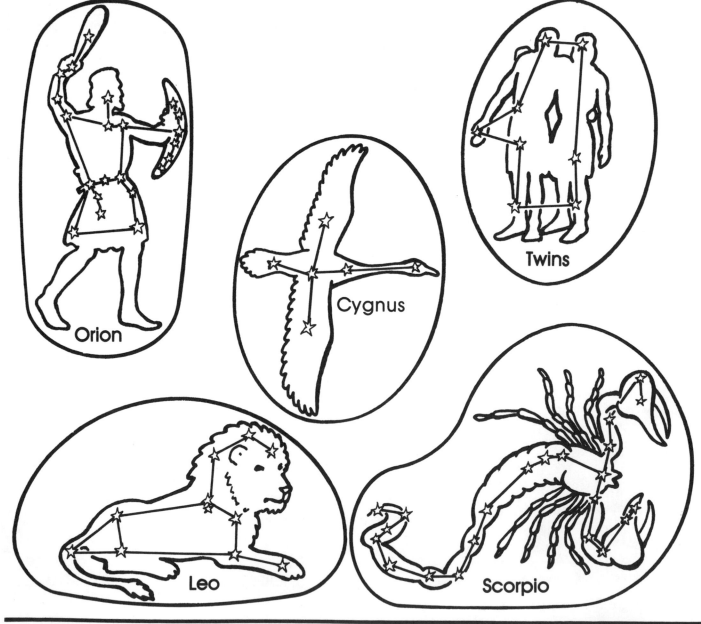

Orion

Cygnus

Twins

Leo

Scorpio

Star Gazer (cover)

Name _____

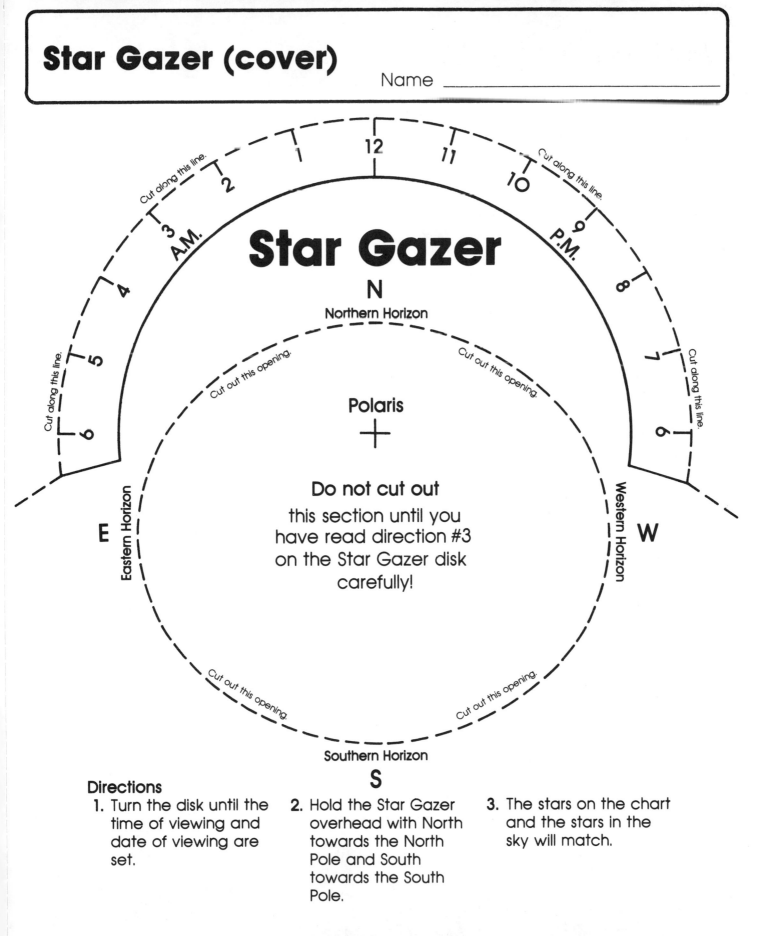

Star Gazer

N

Northern Horizon

Cut out this opening.   Cut out this opening.

Polaris

+

Do not cut out

this section until you have read direction #3 on the Star Gazer disk carefully!

E
Eastern Horizon

Western Horizon
W

Cut out this opening.   Cut out this opening.

Southern Horizon

S

Cut along this line.

A.M.   P.M.

12   1   11
2   10
3   9
4   8
5   7
6   6

Directions

1. Turn the disk until the time of viewing and date of viewing are set.

2. Hold the Star Gazer overhead with North towards the North Pole and South towards the South Pole.

3. The stars on the chart and the stars in the sky will match.

The Star Gazer is made for latitude 40°N., but it will be helpful for any mid-latitude areas in the Northern Hemisphere.

Star Gazer (disk)

Name _____

1. Cut out the Star Gazer disk and the star gazer cover.

2. Lay the cover on an 8 x 11 inch sheet of tagboard (or other sturdy paper). Line up and tape the bottom edge.

3. Make a pin hole through the cover and tagboard at the point marked "Polaris."

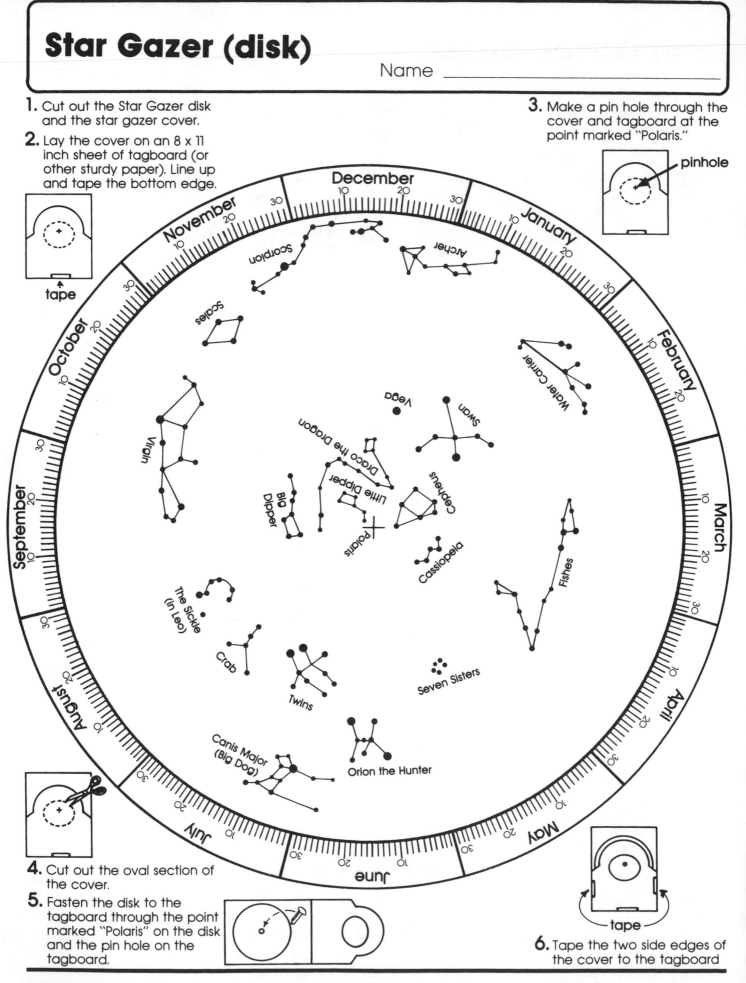

4. Cut out the oval section of the cover.

5. Fasten the disk to the tagboard through the point marked "Polaris" on the disk and the pin hole on the tagboard.

6. Tape the two side edges of the cover to the tagboard

©1992 Instructional Fair, Inc.

IF8758 Science Enrichment

"Lift-off"

Name _____

"3-2-1, lift-off!" With a mighty roar, the Saturn V **rocket** leaves the **launch pad.**

Riding high on top of the Saturn V in the **Command Module** are the three Apollo astronauts. Below their Command Module is a Lunar Landing Module which will land two of the astronauts on the moon's surface.

Below this, the Saturn V has three parts, or **stages.** It takes a lot of power to escape the Earth's pull, called **gravity.** The spacecraft must reach a speed of almost 40,000 km per hour. The bottom, or first stage, is the largest. After each stage uses up its **fuel,** it drops off, and the next stage starts. Each stage has its own fuel and **oxygen.** The fuels need oxygen, otherwise they will not burn.

The astronauts are now on their 3-day journey to the moon.

Color each Saturn V section a different color. Color the key to match each section.

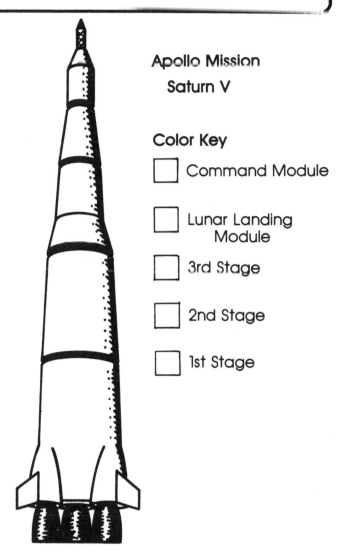

Apollo Mission
Saturn V

Color Key

☐ Command Module

☐ Lunar Landing Module

☐ 3rd Stage

☐ 2nd Stage

☐ 1st Stage

Fill in the spaces with the words in bold from above. Then use the numbered letters to answer the question.

1. The Saturn V __ __ __ __ __ __ has three main parts, or __ __ __ __ __ __.
                    13   1   5

2. Rocket engines burn __ __ __ __ and __ __ __ __ __.
              10   8   6   16   7

3. The Earth's pull is called __ __ __ __ __ __ __.
               16 11   14

4. "Lift-off." The Saturn V leaves the __ __ __ __ __ __ __ __.
                 9   2   12

5. The Apollo astronauts ride in the __ __ __ __ __ __ __ __ __ __ __ __.
                       3 15   4

What were the first words spoken from the surface of the moon on July 20, 1969?

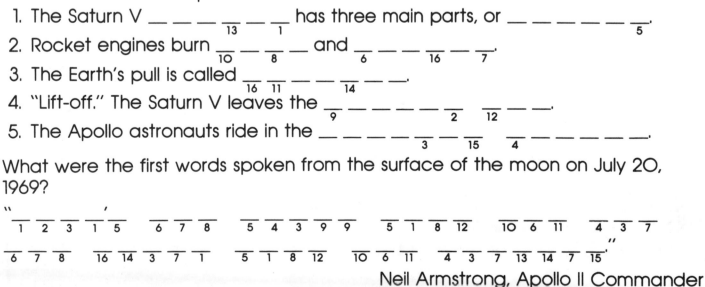

Neil Armstrong, Apollo II Commander

"Live Via Satellite"

Name _____

"This program is brought to you live via satellite from halfway around the world." Satellites are very helpful in sending TV messages from the other side of the world. But this is only one of the special jobs that satellites can do.

Most satellites are placed into orbit around the Earth by riding on top of giant rockets. Only recently some satellites have been carried into orbit by a space shuttle. While orbiting the Earth, the giant doors of the shuttle are opened, and the satellite is pushed into orbit.

This satellite relays T.V. signals from halfway around the world.

Satellites send information about many things. Use the code to find the different kinds of messages and information satellites send.

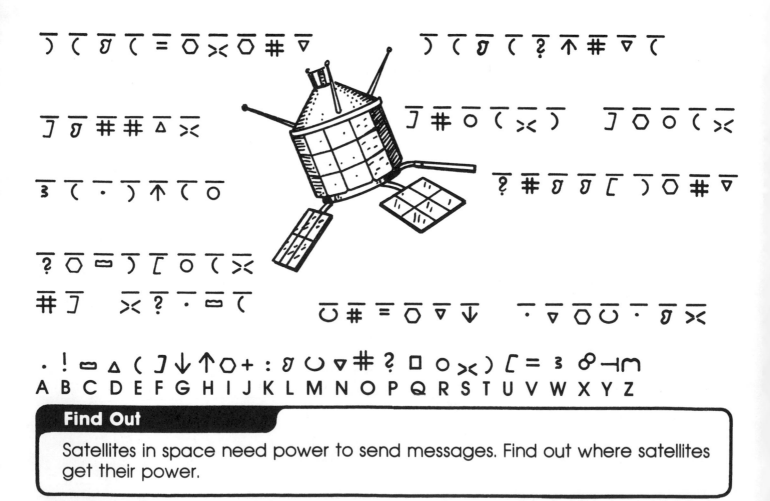

Symbol:	.	!	▱	△	(	⅃	↓	↑	○	+	:	♉	∪	▽	#	?	□	o	⤬	)	⌈	=	₃	8	⊣⋂
Letter:	A	B	C	D	E	F	G	H	I	J	K	L	M	N	O	P	Q	R	S	T	U	V	W	X	Y Z

Find Out

Satellites in space need power to send messages. Find out where satellites get their power.

©1992 Instructional Fair, Inc.

IF8758 Science Enrichment

Terrible Lizard

Name _____

Millions of years ago, dinosaurs may have walked where you live. Now there are no dinosaurs — they are extinct. What were dinosaurs? The word **dinosaur** means "terrible lizard," but dinosaurs were not lizards.

Many scientists think that dinosaurs were reptiles. **Reptiles** are animals that are scaly and lay eggs. Reptiles are cold-blooded. Cold-blooded animals cannot control the temperature of their bodies. Their body temperature is the same temperature as the air around them. This means that if a reptile is in the sun, its body temperature is warm. If the reptile is in the shade, its body temperature is cooler.

• Circle the reptiles in the picture below.

• Help the **Stegosaurus** (steg-uh-SAWR-us) find his dinner. Follow the path of the maze. When you come to a fork in the path, follow the path that describes the characteristics of a reptile.

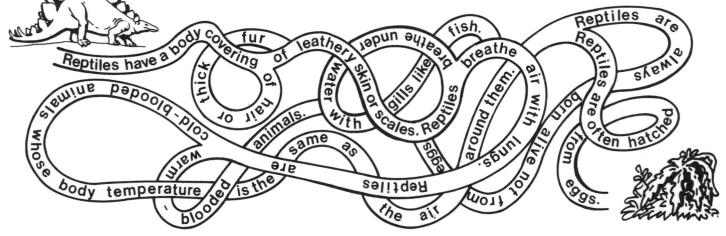

• Circle the **reptile characteristics** on the chart below.

Skin Covering	Young Born	Breathing	Body Temperature
rough skin	eggs	gills	cold-blooded
(or)	(or)	(or)	(or)
feathers	alive	lungs	warm-blooded

©1992 Instructional Fair, Inc.

IF8758 Science Enrichment

Sea Monsters

Name _____

While dinosaurs were living on the earth, large "sea monsters" were living in the sea. These large monsters were not fish. They were reptiles. Most reptiles lay eggs, but the sea monsters gave birth to live young.

• To find out what the three sea monsters below looked like, follow the correct path. The correct path will also give you some interesting facts to help you answer the questions at the bottom of the page.

Plesiosaurs
(PLEEZ-ee-uh-sawrs)

Ichthyosaurs
(IK-thee-uh-sawrs)

Pliosaurs
(PLY-uh-sawrs)

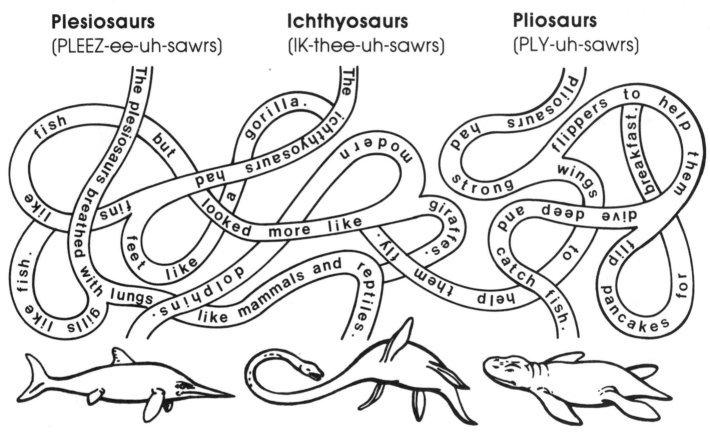

• Circle True (T) or False (F).

T F Plesiosaurs breathed with gills.

T F Ichthyosaurs looked very much like giant dolphins.

T F Most sea monsters laid eggs.

T F Reptiles breathe air with their lungs.

T F Pliosaurs were meat-eating sea monsters.

T F Ichthyosaurs were big fish.

Fun Fact

A young girl found the first complete **Plesiosaur** fossil! Eleven-year-old Mary Anning was walking along the southern coast of England looking for small fossils to sell in order to earn money for her family when she found the fossil.

Dinosaur Names

Name _____

Did you know that most dinosaur names tell us something about the animal? Remember, the word dinosaur means "terrible lizard."

- Some dinosaurs and other prehistoric animals are pictured below. Look at the pictures carefully and then write the correct letter next to the dinosaur name.

Triceratops ( )
(try-SAIR-uh-tops)

Deinonychus ( )
(die-NON-uh-cus)

Stegosaurus ( )
(steg-uh-SAWR-us)

Panoplosaurus ( )
(pan-OP-luh-sawr-us)

Corythosaurus ( )
(co-RITH-uh-sawr-us)

Styracosaurus ( )
(stih-RACK-uh-sawr-us)

Name meanings

A. Plated or Roofed Lizard
B. Fish Lizard
C. Three-horned Face
D. Terrible Claw
E. Duck Lizard
F. Helmet Lizard
G. Armored Lizard
H. Single-horned
I. Spiked Lizard

Anatosaurus ( )
(uh-nat-uh-SAWR-us)

Icthyosaurus ( )
(ik-thee-uh-SAWR-us)

Monoclonius ( )
(mah-no-KLONE-ee-us)

Fantastic Fact

The eggs of a dinosaur were not always safe from other dinosaurs. The **Oviraptor,** or "egg thief," had a birdlike beak which it used to crunch large dinosaur eggs. (ov-uh-RAP-tur)

More Fossils

Name _____

- Besides bone fossils, scientists have found other kinds of fossils. Below are the pictures of some of these other kinds of fossils. Draw a line from the description of the kind of fossil to its picture.

A dinosaur makes footprints in the soft mud. The mud hardens and turns into rock.

Sometimes the skin of a dinosaur is changed into a fossil.

The eggs of some dinosaurs have been changed into fossil eggs.

- Carefully study these dinosaur footprints. Draw a line from the dinosaur to its footprints.

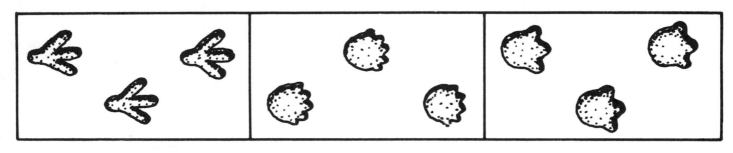

Triceratops   Megalosaurus   Parasaurolophus

Fantastic Fact

Fossil eggs of the **Protoceratops** have been found with the skeletons of tiny baby **Protoceratops** inside! (pro-toe-SAIR-uh-tops)

Nippers, Rippers, and Grinders

Name _____

1.　　　　　　　2.　　　　　　　3.

Scientists tell us that some of the dinosaurs were meat-eaters and others were plant-eaters. But how do the scientists know? By looking at the teeth of certain dinosaur fossils, scientists can tell what those dinosaurs ate. Meat-eaters had sharp, saw-edged teeth (figure 1), for cutting and ripping flesh. Plant-eating dinosaurs had either peg-like teeth (figure 2), for nipping plants, or flat grinding teeth (figure 3), to munch tough twigs or leaves.

1. Match the dinosaur to its teeth by writing its name in the space provided.
2. Circle either "M" for meat-eater or "P" for plant-eater.

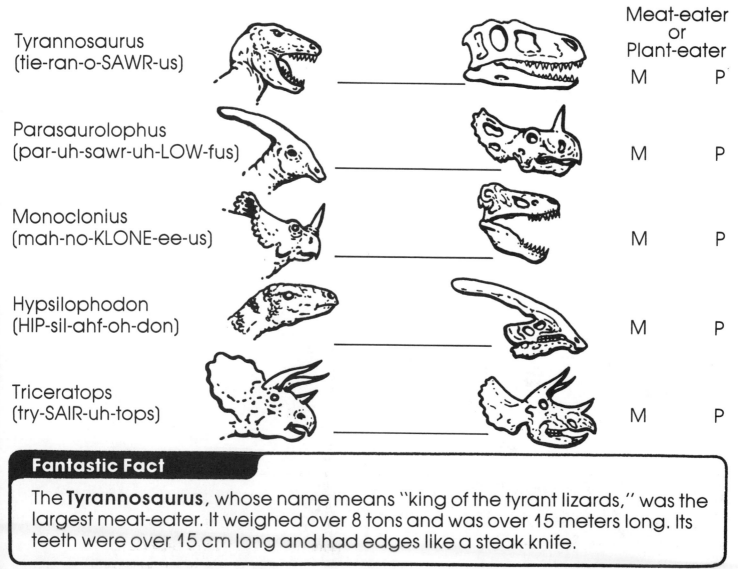

Meat-eater
or
Plant-eater

Tyrannosaurus
(tie-ran-o-SAWR-us)
_____   M   P

Parasaurolophus
(par-uh-sawr-uh-LOW-fus)
_____   M   P

Monoclonius
(mah-no-KLONE-ee-us)
_____   M   P

Hypsilophodon
(HIP-sil-ahf-oh-don)
_____   M   P

Triceratops
(try-SAIR-uh-tops)
_____   M   P

Fantastic Fact

The **Tyrannosaurus**, whose name means "king of the tyrant lizards," was the largest meat-eater. It weighed over 8 tons and was over 15 meters long. Its teeth were over 15 cm long and had edges like a steak knife.

Dinosaur Framework

Name _____

Fossil bones are the only clues we have to tell us what the dinosaurs were like. Small, fast dinosaurs had very lightweight bones that were sometimes hollow. Big, heavy dinosaurs had thick bones to help support all their weight.

Dinosaurs were vertebrates. A **vertebrate** is an animal that has a backbone. A backbone is made of many smaller bones, called **vertebrae.** The vertebrae are connected to each other. Humans and all other mammals, reptiles, birds, fish, and amphibians that live today are vertebrates.

• Match the dinosaurs pictured below with the skeletons by putting the correct number next to each skeleton. Then with a crayon or marker, color the backbone of each dinosaur skeleton.

1. Plateosaurus

2. Brachiosaurus

3. Triceratops

4. Lesothosaurus

5. Tyrannosaurus

6. Spinosaurus

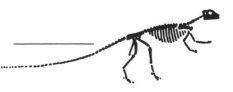

Lumps, Bumps, and Scars

Name _____

It's exciting when a **paleontologist** (a scientist who studies fossils) finds a dinosaur fossil. The fossil might be from a dinosaur no one has ever discoverd before.

It might take years for paleontologists to put together most of a dinosaur's bones. The lumps, bumps, and scars on the bones give them clues as to what the dinosaur might have looked like. These marks on the bones show where muscles were attached. By looking at the whole skeleton and the lumps, bumps, and scars on each bone, paleontologists can carefully guess the shape of the dinosaur's body.

- The two skeletons below are make-believe dinosaurs that nobody has ever found. Study the skeletons. Then use colored pencils, crayons, or markers to draw right over the skeleton, to show what these dinosaurs might have looked like. Name your dinosaurs.

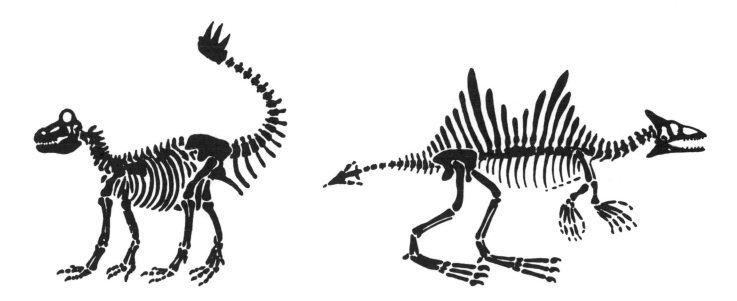

_____   _____

Fun Fact

Not all dinosaurs were huge giants. The **Compsognathus** was the smallest dinosaur. It was about the same size as a crow, and it could run very fast. (komp-SAHG-nay-thus)

©1992 Instructional Fair, Inc.   IF8758 Science Enrichment

Dinosaur Defense

Name _____

How did the plant-eating dinosaurs protect themselves from the attacks of the fierce meat-eating dinosaurs? One way was to travel in groups. But they also had other ways to defend themselves. For example, some had horns and some could run very fast.

- Look at the plant-eating dinosaurs below. Find the features of their bodies that gave them protection from their enemies. Explain in the space provided.

Stegosaurus
(steg-uh-SAWR-us)

_____
_____
_____
_____

Ankylosaurus
(ang-KILE-uh-sawr-us)

_____
_____
_____
_____

Laosaurus
(LAY-uh-sawr-us)

_____
_____
_____

Triceratops
(try-SAIR-uh-tops)

_____
_____
_____
_____

The End of the Dinosaurs

Name _____

What could have killed all the dinosaurs? Scientists are not really sure. They have many different **theories,** or explanations, for why the dinosaurs died out.

- Several theories are listed below. Each theory has a **cause** and an **effect.** A cause is "a change that happened on earth" and an effect is "what resulted from the change on earth." Draw a line from each cause to its effect.

Cause

A huge meteor hit the earth, starting fires and making a thick cloud of dust and smoke that covered the earth.

Small, fast mammals that liked to eat eggs quickly spread around the world.

New kinds of flowering plants started to grow on the earth. These plants had poison in them that the dinosaurs could not taste.

When dinosaurs were living, the earth was warm all year long. Suddenly the earth became cooler with cold winter months.

Effect

Dinosaurs were cold-blooded and they couldn't find places to hibernate. They had no fur or feathers to keep them warm. They froze to death.

The sunlight was blocked and plants couldn't grow. The dinosaurs starved to death.

Fewer and fewer baby dinosaurs were born.

The dinosaurs ate poison without even knowing it and they died.

Dinosaur Mobile

Name _____

1. Color the dinosaurs.
2. Cut out the dinosaurs.
3. Match the dinosaurs with the descriptions below. Write the dinosaur's name on the back of its picture.
4. Assemble the dinosaurs with string and a hanger to make a mobile. (Hint: Your mobile will be stronger if you paste the pictures on tagboard.)

Triceratops: large dinosaur; three horns, one over each eye and one over its nose; large shield of bone protected its neck.

Parasaurolophus: large dinosaur; big crest curved backward from its head to beyond its shoulders.

Tyrannosaurus: giant meat-eater; large head; jaws filled with sharp teeth.

Brontosaurus: giant dinosaur; weighed almost 40 tons; massive body and tail; its front legs were shorter than its hind legs.

Ankylosaurus: body covered with armored plates; large bony club on the end of its tail.

Answer Key

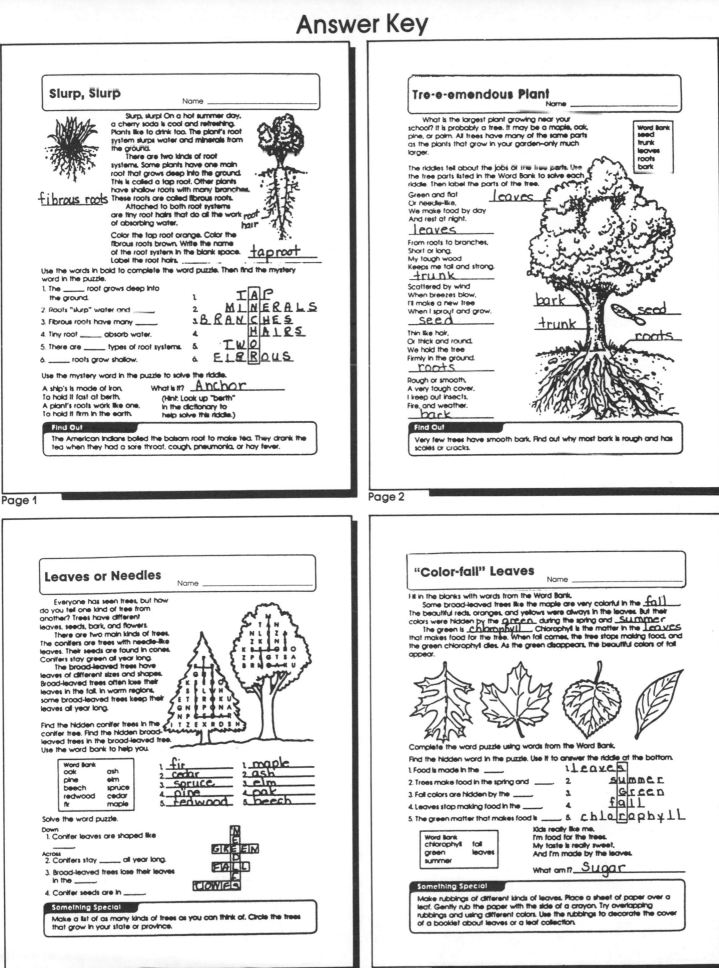

Slurp, Slurp

Name _____

Slurp, slurp! On a hot summer day, a cherry soda is cool and refreshing. Plants like to drink too. The plant's root system slurps water and minerals from the ground.

There are two kinds of root systems. Some plants have one main root that grows deep into the ground. This is called a tap root. Other plants have shallow roots with many branches. These roots are called fibrous roots.

Attached to both root systems are tiny root hairs that do all the work of absorbing water.

fibrous roots

root hair

Color the tap root orange. Color the fibrous roots brown. Write the name of the root system in the blank space. Label the root hairs. _____

taproot

Use the words in bold to complete the word puzzle. Then find the mystery word in the puzzle.

1. The _____ root grows deep into the ground.
2. Roots "slurp" water and _____.
3. Fibrous roots have many _____.
4. Tiny root _____ absorb water.
5. There are _____ types of root systems.
6. _____ roots grow shallow.

1. T A P
2. M I N E R A L S
3. B R A N C H E S
4. H A I R S
5. T W O
6. F I B R O U S

Use the mystery word in the puzzle to solve the riddle.

A ship's is made of iron,
To hold it fast at berth.
A plant's roots work like one,
To hold it firm in the earth.

What is it? Anchor

(Hint: Look up "berth" in the dictionary to help solve this riddle.)

Find Out
The American Indians boiled the balsam root to make tea. They drank the tea when they had a sore throat, cough, pneumonia, or hay fever.

Page 1

Tre-e-emendous Plant

Name _____

What is the largest plant growing near your school? It is probably a tree. It may be a maple, oak, pine, or palm. All trees have many of the same parts as the plants that grow in your garden—only much larger.

Word Bank
seed
trunk
leaves
roots
bark

The riddles tell about the jobs of the tree parts. Use the tree parts listed in the Word Bank to solve each riddle. Then label the parts of the tree.

Green and flat
Or needle-like,
We make food by day
And rest at night.
leaves

leaves

From roots to branches,
Short or long,
My tough wood
Keeps me tall and strong.
trunk

bark

Scattered by wind
When breezes blow,
I'll make a new tree
When I sprout and grow.
seed

seed

trunk

roots

Thin like hair,
Or thick and round,
We hold the tree
Firmly in the ground.
roots

Rough or smooth,
A very tough cover,
I keep out insects,
Fire, and weather.
bark

Find Out
Very few trees have smooth bark. Find out why most bark is rough and has scales or cracks.

Page 2

Leaves or Needles

Name _____

Everyone has seen trees, but how do you tell one kind of tree from another? Trees have different leaves, seeds, bark, and flowers.

There are two main kinds of trees. The conifers are trees with needle-like leaves. Their seeds are found in cones. Conifers stay green all year long.

The broad-leaved trees have leaves of different sizes and shapes. Broad-leaved trees often lose their leaves in the fall. In warm regions, some broad-leaved trees keep their leaves all year long.

Find the hidden conifer trees in the conifer tree. Find the hidden broad-leaved trees in the broad-leaved tree. Use the word bank to help you.

Word Bank
oak   ash
pine   elm
beech   spruce
redwood   cedar
fir   maple

1. fir
2. cedar
3. spruce
4. pine
5. redwood

1. maple
2. ash
3. elm
4. oak
5. beech

Solve the word puzzle.

Down
1. Conifer leaves are shaped like _____

Across
2. Conifers stay _____ all year long.
3. Broad-leaved trees lose their leaves in the _____.
4. Conifer seeds are in _____.

N
E
E
D
G R E E N
L
F A L L
E
C O N E S

Something Special
Make a list of as many kinds of trees as you can think of. Circle the trees that grow in your state or province.

Page 3

"Color-fall" Leaves

Name _____

Fill in the blanks with words from the Word Bank.

Some broad-leaved trees like the maple are very colorful in the fall. The beautiful reds, oranges, and yellows were always in the leaves. But their colors were hidden by the green during the spring and summer.

The green is chlorophyll. Chlorophyll is the matter in the leaves that makes food for the tree. When fall comes, the tree stops making food, and the green chlorophyll dies. As the green disappears, the beautiful colors of fall appear.

Complete the word puzzle using words from the Word Bank.
Find the hidden word in the puzzle. Use it to answer the riddle at the bottom.

1. Food is made in the _____.
2. Trees make food in the spring and _____.
3. Fall colors are hidden by the _____.
4. Leaves stop making food in the _____.
5. The green matter that makes food is _____.

1. l e a v e s
2. s u m m e r
3. g r e e n
4. f a l l
5. c h l o r o p h y l l

Word Bank
chlorophyll   fall
green   leaves
summer

Kids really like me.
I'm food for the trees.
My taste is really sweet.
And I'm made by the leaves.

What am I? Sugar

Something Special
Make rubbings of different kinds of leaves. Place a sheet of paper over a leaf. Gently rub the paper with the side of a crayon. Try overlapping rubbings and using different colors. Use the rubbings to decorate the cover of a booklet about leaves or a leaf collection.

Page 4

Answer Key

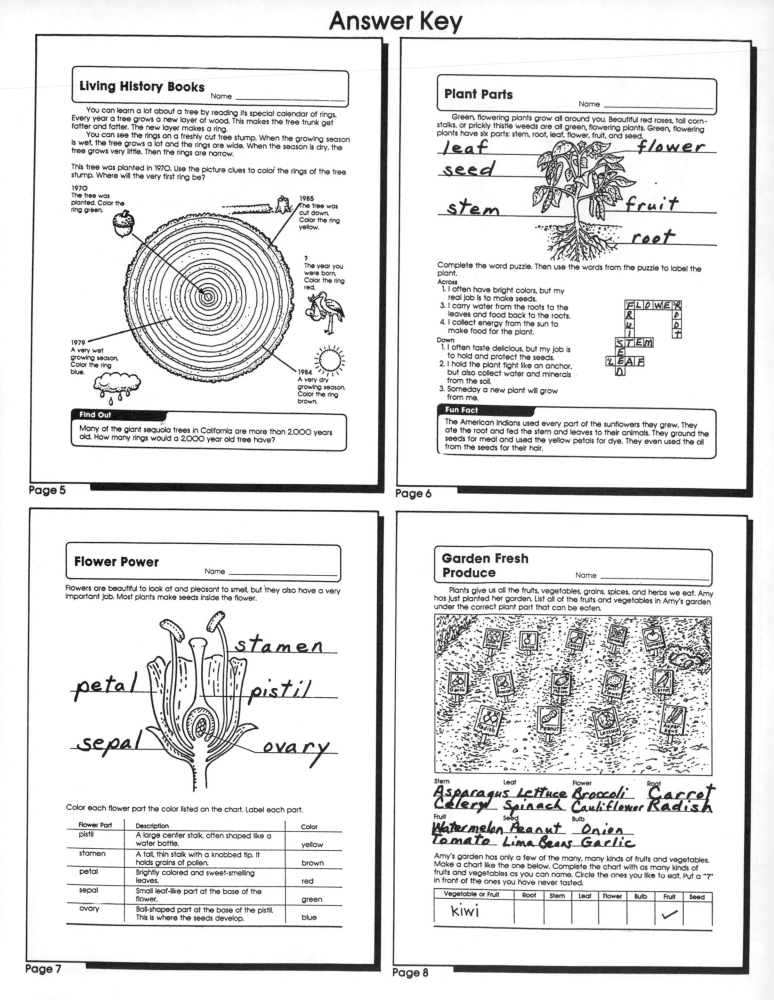

Page 5

Living History Books

Name _____

You can learn a lot about a tree by reading its special calendar of rings. Every year a tree grows a new layer of wood. This makes the tree trunk get fatter and fatter. The new layer makes a ring.

You can see the rings on a freshly cut tree stump. When the growing season is wet, the tree grows a lot and the rings are wide. When the season is dry, the tree grows very little. Then the rings are narrow.

This tree was planted in 1970. Use the picture clues to color the rings of the tree stump. Where will the very first ring be?

1970
The tree was planted. Color the ring green.

1985
The tree was cut down. Color the ring yellow.

?
The year you were born. Color the ring red.

1979
A very wet growing season. Color the ring blue.

1984
A very dry growing season. Color the ring brown.

Find Out

Many of the giant sequoia trees in California are more than 2,000 years old. How many rings would a 2,000 year old tree have?

Page 6

Plant Parts

Name _____

Green, flowering plants grow all around you. Beautiful red roses, tall corn-stalks, or prickly thistle weeds are all green, flowering plants. Green, flowering plants have six parts: stem, root, leaf, flower, fruit, and seed.

leaf

seed

stem

flower

fruit

root

Complete the word puzzle. Then use the words from the puzzle to label the plant.

Across
1. I often have bright colors, but my real job is to make seeds.
3. I carry water from the roots to the leaves and food back to the roots.
4. I collect energy from the sun to make food for the plant.

Down
1. I often taste delicious, but my job is to hold and protect the seeds.
2. I hold the plant tight like an anchor, but also collect water and minerals from the soil.
3. Someday a new plant will grow from me.

F L O W E R
R   O
U   O
I   S T E M
T   E
    E
L E A F
    D

Fun Fact

The American Indians used every part of the sunflowers they grew. They ate the root and fed the stem and leaves to their animals. They ground the seeds for meal and used the yellow petals for dye. They even used the oil from the seeds for their hair.

Page 7

Flower Power

Name _____

Flowers are beautiful to look at and pleasant to smell, but they also have a very important job. Most plants make seeds inside the flower.

stamen

petal

pistil

sepal

ovary

Color each flower part the color listed on the chart. Label each part.

Flower Part	Description	Color
pistil	A large center stalk, often shaped like a water bottle.	yellow
stamen	A tall, thin stalk with a knobbed tip. It holds grains of pollen.	brown
petal	Brightly colored and sweet-smelling leaves.	red
sepal	Small leaf-like part at the base of the flower.	green
ovary	Ball-shaped part at the base of the pistil. This is where the seeds develop.	blue

---

Page 8

Garden Fresh Produce

Name _____

Plants give us all the fruits, vegetables, grains, spices, and herbs we eat. Amy has just planted her garden. List all of the fruits and vegetables in Amy's garden under the correct plant part that can be eaten.

Stem	Leaf	Flower	Root
Asparagus	Lettuce	Broccoli	Carrot
Celery	Spinach	Cauliflower	Radish

Fruit	Seed	Bulb
Watermelon	Peanut	Onion
Tomato	Lima Beans	Garlic

Amy's garden has only a few of the many, many kinds of fruits and vegetables. Make a chart like the one below. Complete the chart with as many kinds of fruits and vegetables as you can name. Circle the ones you like to eat. Put a "?" in front of the ones you have never tasted.

Vegetable or Fruit	Root	Stem	Leaf	Flower	Bulb	Fruit	Seed
kiwi						✓	

Answer Key

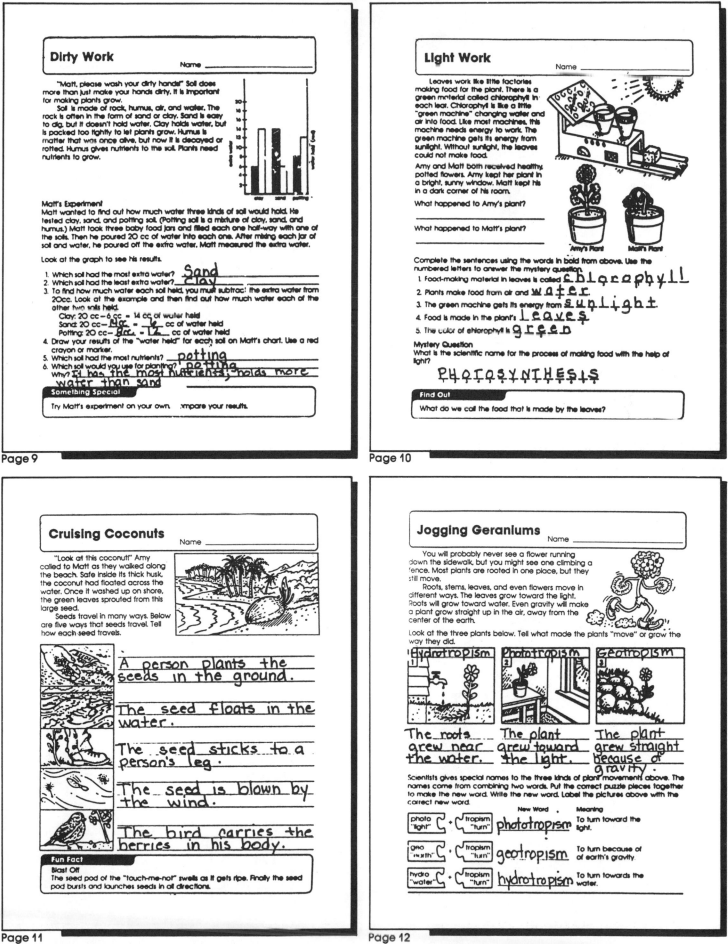

Dirty Work

Name _____

"Matt, please wash your dirty hands!" Soil does more than just make your hands dirty. It is important for making plants grow.

Soil is made of rock, humus, air, and water. The rock is often in the form of sand or clay. Sand is easy to dig, but it doesn't hold water. Clay holds water, but is packed too tightly to let plants grow. Humus is matter that was once alive, but now is decayed or rotted. Humus gives nutrients to the soil. Plants need nutrients to grow.

Matt's Experiment
Matt wanted to find out how much water three kinds of soil would hold. He tested clay, sand, and potting soil. (Potting soil is a mixture of clay, sand, and humus.) Matt took three baby food jars and filled each one half-way with one of the soils. Then he poured 20 cc of water into each one. After mixing each jar of soil and water, he poured off the extra water. Matt measured the extra water.

Look at the graph to see his results.

1. Which soil had the most extra water? __Sand__
2. Which soil had the least extra water? __clay__
3. To find how much water each soil held, you must subtract the extra water from 20cc. Look at the example and then find out how much water each soil the other two soils held.
   Clay: 20 cc – 6 cc = 14 cc of water held
   Sand: 20 cc – __14cc__ = __6__ cc of water held
   Potting: 20 cc – __8cc__ = __12__ cc of water held
4. Draw your results of the "water held" for each soil on Matt's chart. Use a red crayon or marker.
5. Which soil had the most nutrients? __potting__
6. Which soil would you use for planting? __potting__
   Why? __It has the most nutrients; holds more water than sand__

Something Special

Try Matt's experiment on your own. Compare your results.

Light Work

Name _____

Leaves work like little factories making food for the plant. There is a green material called chlorophyll in each leaf. Chlorophyll is like a little "green machine" changing water and air into food. Like most machines, this machine needs energy to work. The green machine gets its energy from sunlight. Without sunlight, the leaves could not make food.

Amy and Matt both received healthy, potted flowers. Amy kept her plant in a bright, sunny window. Matt kept his in a dark corner of his room.

What happened to Amy's plant?

_____

What happened to Matt's plant?

_____

Amy's Plant   Matt's Plant

Complete the sentences using the words in bold from above. Use the numbered letters to answer the mystery question.

1. Food-making material in leaves is called __chlorophyll__
2. Plants make food from air and __water__
3. The green machine gets its energy from __sunlight__
4. Food is made in the plant's __leaves__
5. The color of chlorophyll is __green__

Mystery Question
What is the scientific name for the process of making food with the help of light?

__PHOTOSYNTHESIS__

Find Out

What do we call the food that is made by the leaves?

Cruising Coconuts

Name _____

"Look at this coconut!" Amy called to Matt as they walked along the beach. Safe inside its thick husk, the coconut had floated across the water. Once it washed up on shore, the green leaves sprouted from this large seed.

Seeds travel in many ways. Below are five ways that seeds travel. Tell how each seed travels.

__A person plants the seeds in the ground.__

__The seed floats in the water.__

__The seed sticks to a person's leg.__

__The seed is blown by the wind.__

__The bird carries the berries in his body.__

Fun Fact

Blast Off
The seed pod of the "touch-me-not" swells as it gets ripe. Finally the seed pod bursts and launches seeds in all directions.

Jogging Geraniums

Name _____

You will probably never see a flower running down the sidewalk, but you might see one climbing a fence. Most plants are rooted in one place, but they still move.

Roots, stems, leaves, and even flowers move in different ways. The leaves grow toward the light. Roots will grow toward water. Even gravity will make a plant grow straight up in the air, away from the center of the earth.

Look at the three plants below. Tell what made the plants "move" or grow the way they did.

__Hydrotropism__   __Phototropism__   __Geotropism__

__The roots grew near the water.__   __The plant grew toward the light.__   __The plant grew straight because of gravity.__

Scientists gives special names to the three kinds of plant movements above. The names come from combining two words. Put the correct puzzle pieces together to make the new word. Write the new word. Label the pictures above with the correct new word.

	New Word	Meaning
photo "light" + tropism "turn"	__phototropism__	To turn toward the light.
geo "earth" + tropism "turn"	__geotropism__	To turn because of of earth's gravity.
hydro "water" + tropism "turn"	__hydrotropism__	To turn towards the water.

©1992 Instructional Fair, Inc.   IF8758 Science Enrichment

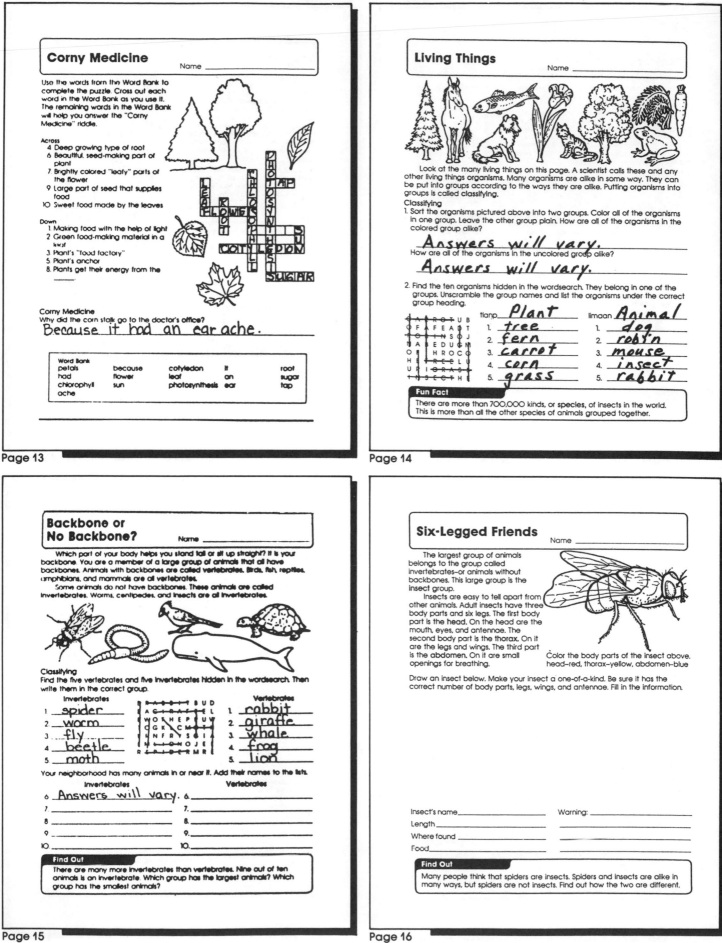

Corny Medicine

Name _____

Use the words from the Word Bank to complete the puzzle. Cross out each word in the Word Bank as you use it. The remaining words in the Word Bank will help you answer the "Corny Medicine" riddle.

Across
4 Deep growing type of root
6 Beautiful, seed-making part of plant
7 Brightly colored "leafy" parts of the flower
9 Large part of seed that supplies food
10 Sweet food made by the leaves

Down
1 Making food with the help of light
2 Green food-making material in a leaf
3 Plant's "food factory"
5 Plant's anchor
8 Plants get their energy from the ____

Corny Medicine
Why did the corn stalk go to the doctor's office?
Because it had an ear ache.

Word Bank

petals	because	cotyledon	it	root
had	flower	leaf	an	sugar
chlorophyll	sun	photosynthesis	ear	tap
ache				

Page 13

Living Things

Name _____

Look at the many living things on this page. A scientist calls these and any other living things organisms. Many organisms are alike in some way. They can be put into groups according to the ways they are alike. Putting organisms into groups is called classifying.

Classifying
1. Sort the organisms pictured above into two groups. Color all of the organisms in one group. Leave the other group plain. How are all of the organisms in the colored group alike?

Answers will vary.

How are all of the organisms in the uncolored group alike?

Answers will vary.

2. Find the ten organisms hidden in the wordsearch. They belong in one of the groups. Unscramble the group names and list the organisms under the correct group heading.

tlanp **Plant**
1. tree
2. fern
3. carrot
4. corn
5. grass

limaan **Animal**
1. dog
2. robin
3. mouse
4. insect
5. rabbit

Fun Fact
There are more than 700,000 kinds, or species, of insects in the world. This is more than all the other species of animals grouped together.

Page 14

Backbone or No Backbone?

Name _____

Which part of your body helps you stand tall or sit up straight? It is your backbone. You are a member of a large group of animals that all have backbones. Animals with backbones are called vertebrates. Birds, fish, reptiles, amphibians, and mammals are all vertebrates.

Some animals do not have backbones. These animals are called invertebrates. Worms, centipedes, and insects are all invertebrates.

Classifying
Find the five vertebrates and five invertebrates hidden in the wordsearch. Then write them in the correct group.

Invertebrates
1. spider
2. worm
3. fly
4. beetle
5. moth

Vertebrates
1. rabbit
2. giraffe
3. whale
4. frog
5. lion

Your neighborhood has many animals in or near it. Add their names to the lists.

Invertebrates
6. Answers will vary.
7. _____
8. _____
9. _____
10. _____

Vertebrates
6. _____
7. _____
8. _____
9. _____
10. _____

Find Out
There are many more invertebrates than vertebrates. Nine out of ten animals is an invertebrate. Which group has the largest animals? Which group has the smallest animals?

Page 15

Six-Legged Friends

Name _____

The largest group of animals belongs to the group called invertebrates—or animals without backbones. This large group is the insect group.

Insects are easy to tell apart from other animals. Adult insects have three body parts and six legs. The first body part is the head. On the head are the mouth, eyes, and antennae. The second body part is the thorax. On it are the legs and wings. The third part is the abdomen. On it are small openings for breathing.

Color the body parts of the insect above. head–red, thorax–yellow, abdomen–blue

Draw an insect below. Make your insect a one-of-a-kind. Be sure it has the correct number of body parts, legs, wings, and antennae. Fill in the information.

Insect's name_____   Warning: _____
Length_____   _____
Where found_____   _____
Food_____   _____

Find Out
Many people think that spiders are insects. Spiders and insects are alike in many ways, but spiders are not insects. Find out how the two are different.

Page 16

Answer Key

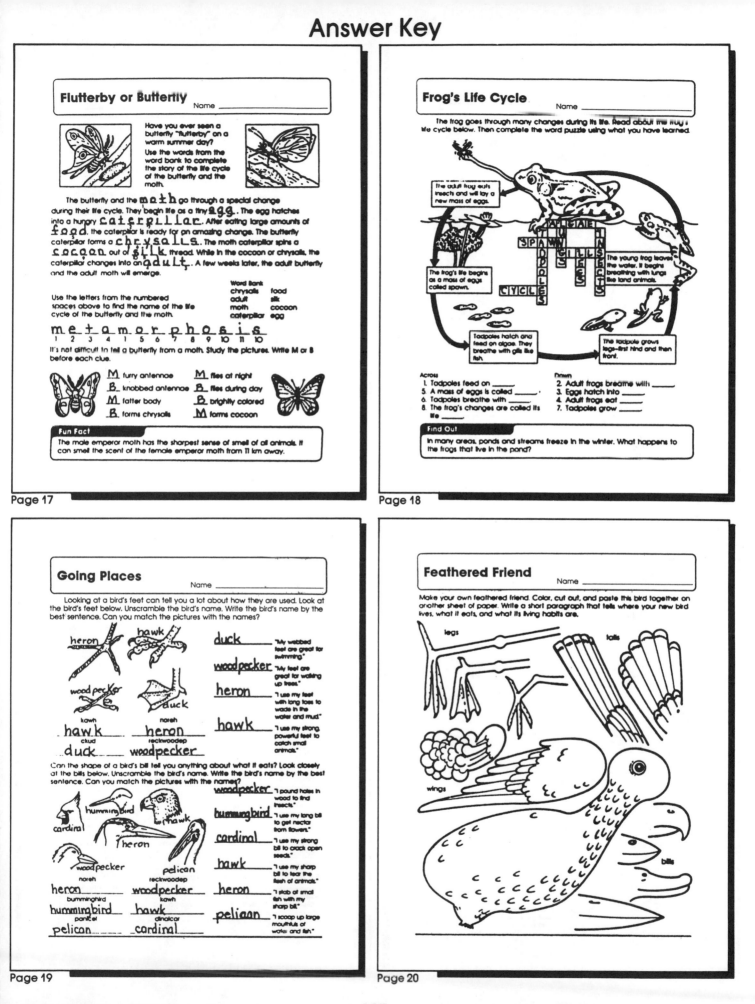

Flutterby or Butterfly

Name _____

Have you ever seen a butterfly "flutterby" on a warm summer day?

Use the words from the word bank to complete the story of the life cycle of the butterfly and the moth.

The butterfly and the **m o t h** go through a special change during their life cycle. They begin life as a tiny **e g g**. The egg hatches into a hungry **c a t e r p i l l a r**. After eating large amounts of **f o o d**, the caterpillar is ready for an amazing change. The butterfly caterpillar forms a **c h r y s a l i s**. The moth caterpillar spins a **c o c o o n** out of **s i l k** thread. While in the cocoon or chrysalis, the caterpillar changes into an **a d u l t**. A few weeks later, the adult butterfly and the adult moth will emerge.

Word Bank
chrysalis   food
adult   silk
moth   cocoon
caterpillar egg

Use the letters from the numbered spaces above to find the name of the life cycle of the butterfly and the moth.

m e t a m o r p h o s i s
1 2 3 4 5 6 7 8 9 10 11 10

It's not difficult to tell a butterfly from a moth. Study the pictures. Write M or B before each clue.

M furry antennae   M flies at night
B knobbed antennae   B flies during day
M fatter body   B brightly colored
B forms chrysalis   M forms cocoon

Fun Fact
The male emperor moth has the sharpest sense of smell of all animals. It can smell the scent of the female emperor moth from 11 km away.

Page 17

Frog's Life Cycle

Name _____

The frog goes through many changes during its life. Read about the frog's life cycle below. Then complete the word puzzle using what you have learned.

The adult frog eats insects and will lay a new mass of eggs.

The frog's life begins as a mass of eggs called spawn.

The young frog leaves the water. It begins breathing with lungs like land animals.

Tadpoles hatch and feed on algae. They breathe with gills like fish.

The tadpole grows legs—first hind and then front.

Across
1. Tadpoles feed on _____.
5. A mass of eggs is called _____.
6. Tadpoles breathe with _____.
8. The frog's changes are called its life _____.

Down
2. Adult frogs breathe with _____.
3. Eggs hatch into _____.
4. Adult frogs eat _____.
7. Tadpoles grow _____.

Find Out
In many areas, ponds and streams freeze in the winter. What happens to the frogs that live in the pond?

Page 18

Going Places

Name _____

Looking at a bird's feet can tell you a lot about how they are used. Look at the bird's feet below. Unscramble the bird's name. Write the bird's name by the best sentence. Can you match the pictures with the names?

heron   hawk

woodpecker   duck
kawn   noreh

hawk   heron
ckud   reckwoodep

duck   woodpecker

duck "My webbed feet are great for swimming."

woodpecker "My feet are great for walking up trees."

heron "I use my feet with long toes to wade in the water and mud."

hawk "I use my strong, powerful feet to catch small animals."

Can the shape of a bird's bill tell you anything about what it eats? Look closely at the bills below. Unscramble the bird's name. Write the bird's name by the best sentence. Can you match the pictures with the names?

hummingbird
cardinal   hawk

heron

woodpecker   pelican
noreh   reckwoodep

heron   woodpecker
bumminghird   kawn

hummingbird   hawk
panicel   dinalcar

pelican   cardinal

woodpecker "I pound holes in wood to find insects."

hummingbird "I use my long bill to get nectar from flowers."

cardinal "I use my strong bill to crack open seeds."

hawk "I use my sharp bill to tear the flesh of animals."

heron "I stab at small fish with my sharp bill."

pelican "I scoop up large mouthfuls of water and fish."

Page 19

Feathered Friend

Name _____

Make your own feathered friend. Color, cut out, and paste this bird together on another sheet of paper. Write a short paragraph that tells where your new bird lives, what it eats, and what its living habits are.

legs   tails

wings

bills

Page 20

Answer Key

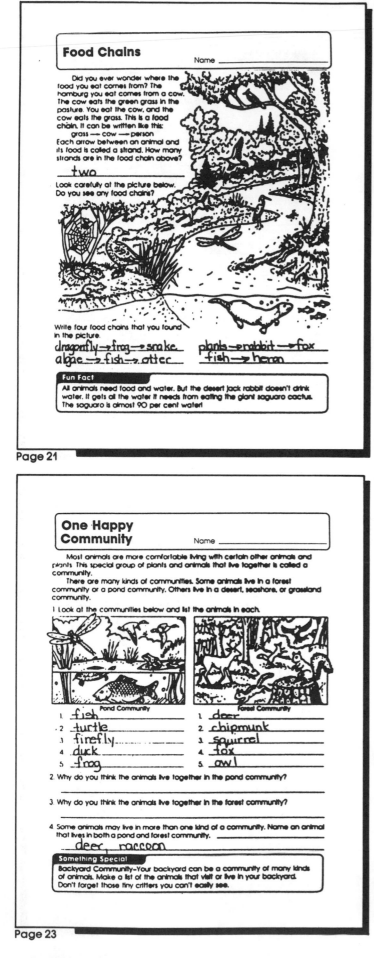

Food Chains

Name _____

Did you ever wonder where the food you eat comes from? The hamburg you eat comes from a cow. The cow eats the green grass in the pasture. You eat the cow, and the cow eats the grass. This is a food chain. It can be written like this:

grass —— cow —— person

Each arrow between an animal and its food is called a strand. How many strands are in the food chain above?

__two__

Look carefully at the picture below. Do you see any food chains?

Write four food chains that you found in the picture.

dragonfly → frog → snake   plants → rabbit → fox

algae → fish → otter   fish → heron

Fun Fact

All animals need food and water. But the desert jack rabbit doesn't drink water. It gets all the water it needs from eating the giant saguaro cactus. The saguaro is almost 90 per cent water!

Page 21

Food Chain Mobile

Name _____

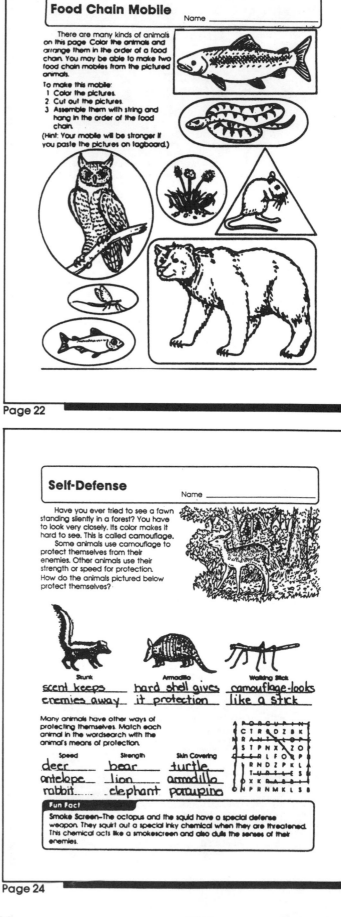

There are many kinds of animals on this page. Color the animals and arrange them in the order of a food chain. You may be able to make two food chain mobiles from the pictured animals.

To make this mobile:
1. Color the pictures.
2. Cut out the pictures.
3. Assemble them with string and hang in the order of the food chain.

(Hint: Your mobile will be stronger if you paste the pictures on tagboard.)

Page 22

One Happy Community

Name _____

Most animals are more comfortable living with certain other animals and plants. This special group of plants and animals that live together is called a community.

There are many kinds of communities. Some animals live in a forest community or a pond community. Others live in a desert, seashore, or grassland community.

1. Look at the communities below and list the animals in each.

Pond Community
1. fish
2. turtle
3. firefly
4. duck
5. frog

Forest Community
1. deer
2. chipmunk
3. squirrel
4. fox
5. owl

2. Why do you think the animals live together in the pond community?

_____

3. Why do you think the animals live together in the forest community?

_____

4. Some animals may live in more than one kind of a community. Name an animal that lives in both a pond and forest community. _____

deer, raccoon

Something Special

Backyard Community–Your backyard can be a community of many kinds of animals. Make a list of the animals that visit or live in your backyard. Don't forget those tiny critters you can't easily see.

Page 23

Self-Defense

Name _____

Have you ever tried to see a fawn standing silently in a forest? You have to look very closely. Its color makes it hard to see. This is called camouflage.

Some animals use camouflage to protect themselves from their enemies. Other animals use their strength or speed for protection. How do the animals pictured below protect themselves?

Skunk
scent keeps enemies away

Armadillo
hard shell gives it protection

Walking Stick
camouflage–looks like a stick

Many animals have other ways of protecting themselves. Match each animal in the wordsearch with the animal's means of protection.

Speed
deer
antelope
rabbit

Strength
bear
lion
elephant

Skin Covering
turtle
armadillo
porcupine

Fun Fact

Smoke Screen–The octopus and the squid have a special defense weapon. They squirt out a special inky chemical when they are threatened. This chemical acts like a smokescreen and also dulls the senses of their enemies.

Page 24

©1992 Instructional Fair, Inc.   108   IF8758 Science Enrichment

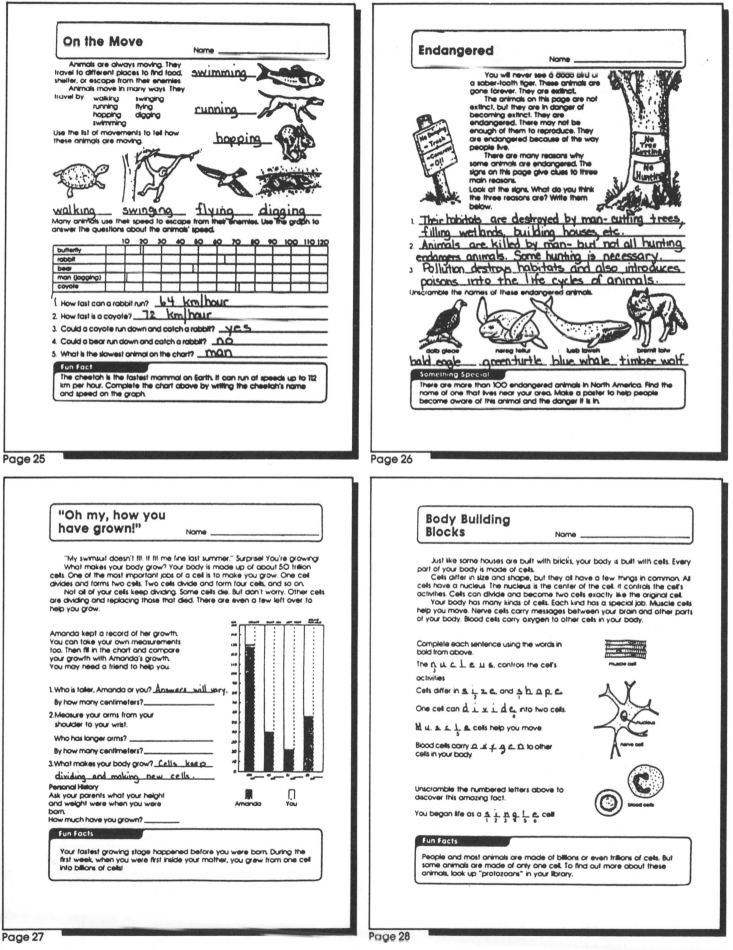

On the Move

Name _____

Animals are always moving. They travel to different places to find food, shelter, or escape from their enemies.

Animals move in many ways. They travel by:
walking   swinging
running   flying
hopping   digging
swimming

swimming
running
hopping

Use the list of movements to tell how these animals are moving.

walking   swinging   flying   digging

Many animals use their speed to escape from their enemies. Use the graph to answer the questions about the animals' speed.

	10	20	30	40	50	60	70	80	90	100	110	120
butterfly												
rabbit												
bear												
man (jogging)												
coyote												

1. How fast can a rabbit run? __64 km/hour__
2. How fast is a coyote? __72 km/hour__
3. Could a coyote run down and catch a rabbit? __yes__
4. Could a bear run down and catch a rabbit? __no__
5. What is the slowest animal on the chart? __man__

Fun Fact
The cheetah is the fastest mammal on Earth. It can run at speeds up to 112 km per hour. Complete the chart above by writing the cheetah's name and speed on the graph.

Page 25

Endangered

Name _____

You will never see a dodo bird or a saber-tooth tiger. These animals are gone forever. They are extinct.

The animals on this page are not extinct, but they are in danger of becoming extinct. They are endangered. There may not be enough of them to reproduce. They are endangered because of the way people live.

There are many reasons why some animals are endangered. The signs on this page give clues to three main reasons.

Look at the signs. What do you think the three reasons are? Write them below.

1. Their habitats are destroyed by man- cutting trees, filling wetlands, building houses, etc.
2. Animals are killed by man- but not all hunting endangers animals. Some hunting is necessary.
3. Pollution destroys habitats and also introduces poisons into the life cycles of animals.

Unscramble the names of these endangered animals.

dalb glece   nereg tellus   lusb lewah   bremil tolw
bald eagle   green turtle   blue whale   timber wolf

Something Special
There are more than 100 endangered animals in North America. Find the name of one that lives near your area. Make a poster to help people become aware of this animal and the danger it is in.

Page 26

"Oh my, how you have grown!"

Name _____

"My swimsuit doesn't fit. It fit me fine last summer." Surprise! You're growing!

What makes your body grow? Your body is made up of about 50 trillion cells. One of the most important jobs of a cell is to make you grow. One cell divides and forms two cells. Two cells divide and form four cells, and so on.

Not all of your cells keep dividing. Some cells die. But don't worry. Other cells are dividing and replacing those that died. There are even a few left over to help you grow.

Amanda kept a record of her growth. You can take your own measurements too. Then fill in the chart and compare your growth with Amanda's growth. You may need a friend to help you.

1. Who is taller, Amanda or you? __Answers will vary.__
   By how many centimeters? _____

2. Measure your arms from your shoulder to your wrist.
   Who has longer arms? _____
   By how many centimeters? _____

3. What makes your body grow? __Cells keep dividing and making new cells.__

Personal History
Ask your parents what your height and weight were when you were born.
How much have you grown? _____

Amanda   You

Fun Facts
Your fastest growing stage happened before you were born. During the first week, when you were first inside your mother, you grew from one cell into billions of cells!

Page 27

Body Building Blocks

Name _____

Just like some houses are built with bricks, your body is built with cells. Every part of your body is made of cells.

Cells differ in size and shape, but they all have a few things in common. All cells have a nucleus. The nucleus is the center of the cell. It controls the cell's activities. Cells can divide and become two cells exactly like the original cell.

Your body has many kinds of cells. Each kind has a special job. Muscle cells help you move. Nerve cells carry messages between your brain and other parts of your body. Blood cells carry oxygen to other cells in your body.

Complete each sentence using the words in bold from above.

The __n u c l e u s__ controls the cell's activities

Cells differ in __s i z e__ and __s h a p e__.

One cell can __d i v i d e__ into two cells.

__M u s c l e__ cells help you move.

Blood cells carry __o x y g e n__ to other cells in your body.

muscle cell

nucleus

nerve cell

blood cells

Unscramble the numbered letters above to discover this amazing fact.

You began life as a __s i n g l e__ cell.

Fun Facts
People and most animals are made of billions or even trillions of cells. But some animals are made of only one cell. To find out more about these animals, look up "protozoans" in your library.

Page 28

Answer Key

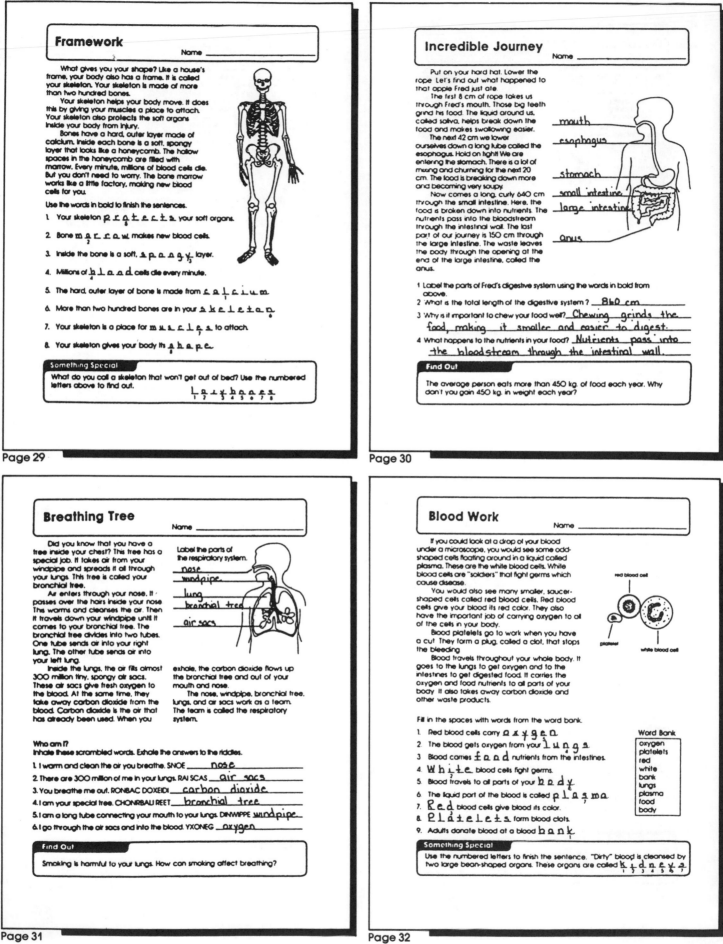

Framework

Name _____

What gives you your shape? Like a house's frame, your body also has a frame. It is called your skeleton. Your skeleton is made of more than two hundred bones.

Your skeleton helps your body move. It does this by giving your muscles a place to attach. Your skeleton also protects the soft organs inside your body from injury.

Bones have a hard, outer layer made of calcium. Inside each bone is a soft, spongy layer that looks like a honeycomb. The hollow spaces in the honeycomb are filled with marrow. Every minute, millions of blood cells die. But you don't need to worry. The bone marrow works like a little factory, making new blood cells for you.

Use the words in bold to finish the sentences.

1. Your skeleton p r o t e c t s your soft organs.
2. Bone m a r r o w makes new blood cells.
3. Inside the bone is a soft, s p o n g y layer.
4. Millions of b l o o d cells die every minute.
5. The hard, outer layer of bone is made from c a l c i u m
6. More than two hundred bones are in your s k e l e t o n
7. Your skeleton is a place for m u s c l e s to attach.
8. Your skeleton gives your body its s h a p e

Something Special

What do you call a skeleton that won't get out of bed? Use the numbered letters above to find out.

L a z y b o n e s

Page 29

Incredible Journey

Name _____

Put on your hard hat. Lower the rope. Let's find out what happened to that apple Fred just ate.

The first 8 cm of rope takes us through Fred's mouth. Those big teeth grind his food. The liquid around us, called saliva, helps break down the food and makes swallowing easier.

The next 42 cm we lower ourselves down a long tube called the esophagus. Hold on tight! We are entering the stomach. There is a lot of mixing and churning for the next 20 cm. The food is breaking down more and becoming very soupy.

Now comes a long, curly 640 cm through the small intestine. Here, the food is broken down into nutrients. The nutrients pass into the bloodstream through the intestinal wall. The last part of our journey is 150 cm through the large intestine. The waste leaves the body through the opening at the end of the large intestine, called the anus.

mouth
esophagus
stomach
small intestine
large intestine
anus

1. Label the parts of Fred's digestive system using the words in bold from above.
2. What is the total length of the digestive system? 860 cm
3. Why is it important to chew your food well? Chewing grinds the food, making it smaller and easier to digest.
4. What happens to the nutrients in your food? Nutrients pass into the bloodstream through the intestinal wall.

Find Out

The average person eats more than 450 kg. of food each year. Why don't you gain 450 kg. in weight each year?

Page 30

Breathing Tree

Name _____

Did you know that you have a tree inside your chest? This tree has a special job. It takes air from your windpipe and spreads it all through your lungs. This tree is called your bronchial tree.

Air enters through your nose. It passes over the hairs inside your nose. This warms and cleanses the air. Then it travels down your windpipe until it comes to your bronchial tree. The bronchial tree divides into two tubes. One tube sends air into your right lung. The other tube sends air into your left lung.

Inside the lungs, the air fills almost 300 million tiny, spongy air sacs. These air sacs give fresh oxygen to the blood. At the same time, they take away carbon dioxide from the blood. Carbon dioxide is the air that has already been used. When you exhale, the carbon dioxide flows up the bronchial tree and out of your mouth and nose.

The nose, windpipe, bronchial tree, lungs, and air sacs work as a team. The team is called the respiratory system.

Label the parts of the respiratory system.

nose
windpipe
lung
bronchial tree
air sacs

Who am I?
Inhale these scrambled words. Exhale the answers to the riddles.

1. I warm and clean the air you breathe. SNOE nose
2. There are 300 million of me in your lungs. RAI SCAS air sacs
3. You breathe me out. RONBAC DOXEIDI carbon dioxide
4. I am your special tree. CHONRBALI REET bronchial tree
5. I am a long tube connecting your mouth to your lungs. DINWIPPE windpipe
6. I go through the air sacs and into the blood. YXONEG oxygen

Find Out

Smoking is harmful to your lungs. How can smoking affect breathing?

Page 31

Blood Work

Name _____

If you could look at a drop of your blood under a microscope, you would see some odd-shaped cells floating around in a liquid called plasma. These are the white blood cells. White blood cells are "soldiers" that fight germs which cause disease.

You would also see many smaller, saucer-shaped cells called red blood cells. Red blood cells give your blood its red color. They also have the important job of carrying oxygen to all of the cells in your body.

Blood platelets go to work when you have a cut. They form a plug, called a clot, that stops the bleeding.

Blood travels throughout your whole body. It goes to the lungs to get oxygen and to the intestines to get digested food. It carries the oxygen and food nutrients to all parts of your body. It also takes away carbon dioxide and other waste products.

red blood cell
platelet
white blood cell

Fill in the spaces with words from the word bank.

1. Red blood cells carry o x y g e n
2. The blood gets oxygen from your l u n g s
3. Blood carries f o o d nutrients from the intestines.
4. W h i t e blood cells fight germs.
5. Blood travels to all parts of your b o d y
6. The liquid part of the blood is called p l a s m a
7. R e d blood cells give blood its color.
8. P l a t e l e t s form blood clots.
9. Adults donate blood at a blood b a n k

Word Bank
oxygen
platelets
red
white
bank
lungs
plasma
food
body

Something Special

Use the numbered letters to finish the sentence. "Dirty" blood is cleansed by two large bean-shaped organs. These organs are called K i d n e y s

Page 32

Answer Key

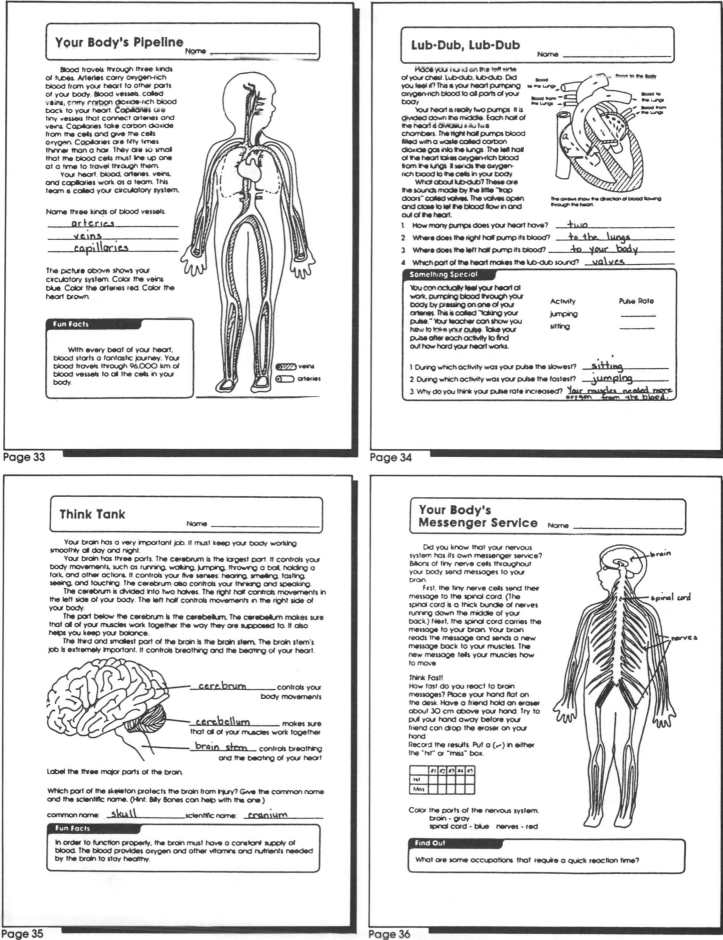

Your Body's Pipeline
Name _____

Blood travels through three kinds of tubes. Arteries carry oxygen-rich blood from your heart to other parts of your body. Blood vessels, called veins, carry carbon dioxide-rich blood back to your heart. Capillaries are tiny vessels that connect arteries and veins. Capillaries take carbon dioxide from the cells and give the cells oxygen. Capillaries are fifty times thinner than a hair. They are so small that the blood cells must line up one at a time to travel through them.

Your heart, blood, arteries, veins, and capillaries work as a team. This team is called your circulatory system.

Name three kinds of blood vessels.

arteries

veins

capillaries

The picture above shows your circulatory system. Color the veins blue. Color the arteries red. Color the heart brown.

Fun Facts
With every beat of your heart, blood starts a fantastic journey. Your blood travels through 96,000 km of blood vessels to all the cells in your body.

▨▨ veins

◯ arteries

Lub-Dub, Lub-Dub
Name _____

Place your hand on the left side of your chest. Lub-dub, lub-dub. Did you feel it? This is your heart pumping oxygen-rich blood to all parts of your body.

Your heart is really two pumps. It is divided down the middle. Each half of the heart is divided into two chambers. The right half pumps blood filled with a waste called carbon dioxide gas into the lungs. The left half of the heart takes oxygen-rich blood from the lungs. It sends the oxygen-rich blood to the cells in your body.

What about lub-dub? These are the sounds made by the little "trap doors" called valves. The valves open and close to let the blood flow in and out of the heart.

The arrows show the direction of blood flowing through the heart.

1. How many pumps does your heart have? _two_
2. Where does the right half pump its blood? _to the lungs_
3. Where does the left half pump its blood? _to your body_
4. Which part of the heart makes the lub-dub sound? _valves_

Something Special
You can actually feel your heart at work, pumping blood through your body by pressing on one of your arteries. This is called "taking your pulse." Your teacher can show you how to take your pulse. Take your pulse after each activity to find out how hard your heart works.

Activity	Pulse Rate
jumping	_____
sitting	_____

1. During which activity was your pulse the slowest? _sitting_
2. During which activity was your pulse the fastest? _jumping_
3. Why do you think your pulse rate increased? _Your muscles needed more oxygen from the blood._

Think Tank
Name _____

Your brain has a very important job. It must keep your body working smoothly all day and night.

Your brain has three parts. The cerebrum is the largest part. It controls your body movements, such as running, walking, jumping, throwing a ball, holding a fork, and other actions. It controls your five senses: hearing, smelling, tasting, seeing, and touching. The cerebrum also controls your thinking and speaking.

The cerebrum is divided into two halves. The right half controls movements in the left side of your body. The left half controls movements in the right side of your body.

The part below the cerebrum is the cerebellum. The cerebellum makes sure that all of your muscles work together the way they are supposed to. It also helps you keep your balance.

The third and smallest part of the brain is the brain stem. The brain stem's job is extremely important. It controls breathing and the beating of your heart.

cerebrum — controls your body movements

cerebellum — makes sure that all of your muscles work together

brain stem — controls breathing and the beating of your heart

Label the three major parts of the brain.

Which part of the skeleton protects the brain from injury? Give the common name and the scientific name. (Hint: Billy Bones can help with this one.)

common name: _skull_   scientific name: _cranium_

Fun Facts
In order to function properly, the brain must have a constant supply of blood. The blood provides oxygen and other vitamins and nutrients needed by the brain to stay healthy.

Your Body's Messenger Service
Name _____

Did you know that your nervous system has its own messenger service? Billions of tiny nerve cells throughout your body send messages to your brain.

First, the tiny nerve cells send their message to the spinal cord. (The spinal cord is a thick bundle of nerves running down the middle of your back.) Next, the spinal cord carries the message to your brain. Your brain reads the message and sends a new message back to your muscles. The new message tells your muscles how to move.

brain

spinal cord

nerves

Think Fast!
How fast do you react to brain messages? Place your hand flat on the desk. Have a friend hold an eraser about 30 cm above your hand. Try to pull your hand away before your friend can drop the eraser on your hand.
Record the results. Put a (✓) in either the "hit" or "miss" box.

	#1	#2	#3	#4	#5
Hit					
Miss					

Color the parts of the nervous system.
brain - gray
spinal cord - blue   nerves - red

Find Out
What are some occupations that require a quick reaction time?

Answer Key

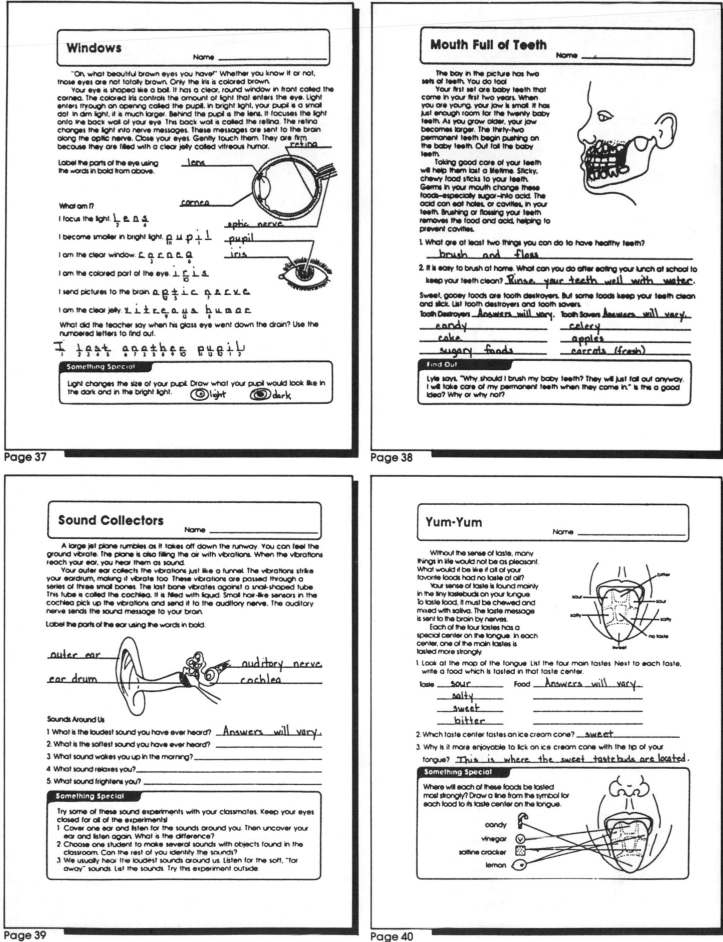

Windows

Name _____

"Oh, what beautiful brown eyes you have!" Whether you know it or not, those eyes are not totally brown. Only the iris is colored brown.

Your eye is shaped like a ball. It has a clear, round window in front called the cornea. The colored iris controls the amount of light that enters the eye. Light enters through an opening called the pupil. In bright light, your pupil is a small dot. In dim light, it is much larger. Behind the pupil is the lens. It focuses the light onto the back wall of your eye. This back wall is called the retina. The retina changes the light into nerve messages. These messages are sent to the brain along the optic nerve. Close your eyes. Gently touch them. They are firm because they are filled with a clear jelly called vitreous humor.

Label the parts of the eye using the words in bold from above.

retina
lens
cornea
optic nerve
pupil
iris

What am I?

I focus the light. **l e n s**

I become smaller in bright light. **p u p i l**

I am the clear window. **c o r n e a**

I am the colored part of the eye. **i r i s**

I send pictures to the brain. **o p t i c n e r v e**

I am the clear jelly. **v i t r e o u s h u m o r**

What did the teacher say when his glass eye went down the drain? Use the numbered letters to find out.

I lost another pupil

Something Special

Light changes the size of your pupil. Draw what your pupil would look like in the dark and in the bright light.   light   dark

---

Mouth Full of Teeth

Name _____

The boy in the picture has two sets of teeth. You do too!

Your first set are baby teeth that come in your first two years. When you are young, your jaw is small. It has just enough room for the twenty baby teeth. As you grow older, your jaw becomes larger. The thirty-two permanent teeth begin pushing on the baby teeth. Out fall the baby teeth.

Taking good care of your teeth will help them last a lifetime. Sticky, chewy food sticks to your teeth. Germs in your mouth change these foods—especially sugar—into acid. The acid can eat holes, or cavities, in your teeth. Brushing or flossing your teeth removes the food and acid, helping to prevent cavities.

1. What are at least two things you can do to have healthy teeth?
   brush and floss

2. It is easy to brush at home. What can you do after eating your lunch at school to keep your teeth clean? **Rinse your teeth well with water.**

Sweet, gooey foods are tooth destroyers. But some foods keep your teeth clean and slick. List tooth destroyers and tooth savers.

Tooth Destroyers **Answers will vary.**   Tooth Savers **Answers will vary.**
candy   **celery**
cake   **apples**
sugary foods   **carrots (fresh)**

Find Out

Lyle says, "Why should I brush my baby teeth? They will just fall out anyway. I will take care of my permanent teeth when they come in." Is this a good idea? Why or why not?

Sound Collectors

Name _____

A large jet plane rumbles as it takes off down the runway. You can feel the ground vibrate. The plane is also filling the air with vibrations. When the vibrations reach your ear, you hear them as sound.

Your outer ear collects the vibrations just like a funnel. The vibrations strike your eardrum, making it vibrate too. These vibrations are passed through a series of three small bones. The last bone vibrates against a snail-shaped tube. This tube is called the cochlea. It is filled with liquid. Small hair-like sensors in the cochlea pick up the vibrations and send it to the auditory nerve. The auditory nerve sends the sound message to your brain.

Label the parts of the ear using the words in bold.

outer ear
ear drum
auditory nerve
cochlea

Sounds Around Us

1. What is the loudest sound you have ever heard? **Answers will vary.**
2. What is the softest sound you have ever heard? _____
3. What sound wakes you up in the morning? _____
4. What sound relaxes you? _____
5. What sound frightens you? _____

Something Special

Try some of these sound experiments with your classmates. Keep your eyes closed for all of the experiments!
1. Cover one ear and listen for the sounds around you. Then uncover your ear and listen again. What is the difference?
2. Choose one student to make several sounds with objects found in the classroom. Can the rest of you identify the sounds?
3. We usually hear the loudest sounds around us. Listen for the soft, "far away" sounds. List the sounds. Try this experiment outside.

Yum-Yum

Name _____

Without the sense of taste, many things in life would not be as pleasant. What would it be like if all of your favorite foods had no taste at all?

Your sense of taste is found mainly in the tiny tastebuds on your tongue. To taste food, it must be chewed and mixed with saliva. The taste message is sent to the brain by nerves.

Each of the four tastes has a special center on the tongue. In each center, one of the main tastes is tasted more strongly.

bitter
sour
sour
salty
salty
no taste
sweet

1. Look at the map of the tongue. List the four main tastes. Next to each taste, write a food which is tasted in that taste center.

   Taste **sour**   Food **Answers will vary**
   salty   _____
   sweet   _____
   bitter   _____

2. Which taste center tastes an ice cream cone? **sweet**

3. Why is it more enjoyable to lick an ice cream cone with the tip of your tongue? **This is where the sweet tastebuds are located.**

Something Special

Where will each of these foods be tasted most strongly? Draw a line from the symbol for each food to its taste center on the tongue.

candy
vinegar
saltine cracker
lemon

©1992 Instructional Fair, Inc.   112   IF8758 Science Enrichment

Answer Key

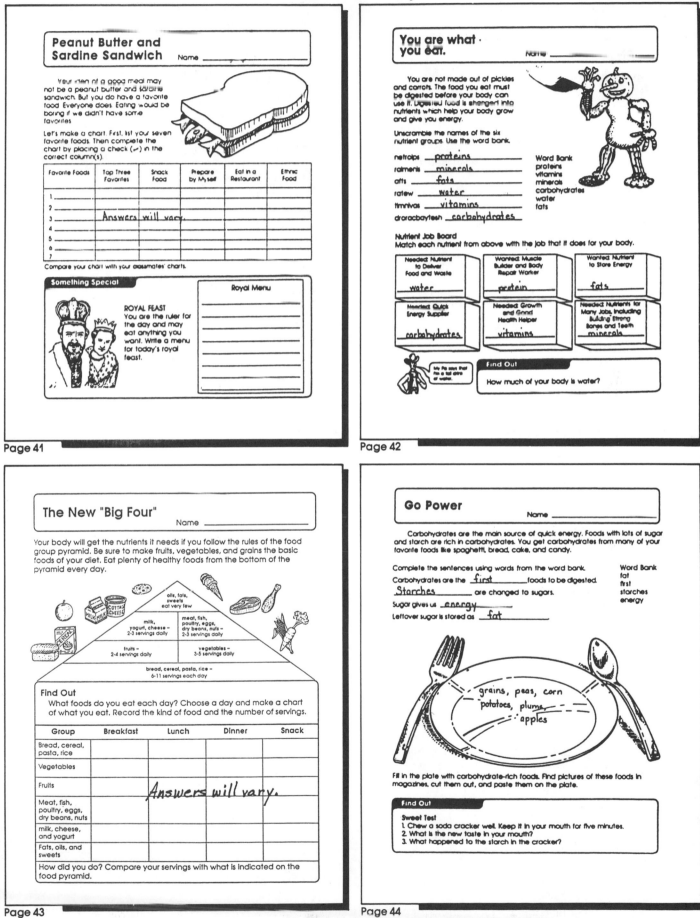

Peanut Butter and Sardine Sandwich

Name _____

Your idea of a good meal may not be a peanut butter and sardine sandwich. But you do have a favorite food. Everyone does. Eating would be boring if we didn't have some favorites.

Let's make a chart. First, list your seven favorite foods. Then complete the chart by placing a check (✓) in the correct column(s).

Favorite Foods	Top Three Favorites	Snack Food	Prepare by Myself	Eat in a Restaurant	Ethnic Food
1 ____					
2 ____					
3 ____	Answers will vary.				
4 ____					
5 ____					
6 ____					
7 ____					

Compare your chart with your classmates' charts.

Something Special

ROYAL FEAST
You are the ruler for the day and may eat anything you want. Write a menu for today's royal feast.

Royal Menu
_____
_____
_____
_____
_____
_____
_____

Page 41

You are what you eat.

Name _____

You are not made out of pickles and carrots. The food you eat must be digested before your body can use it. Digested food is changed into nutrients which help your body grow and give you energy.

Unscramble the names of the six nutrient groups. Use the word bank.

netrolps	**proteins**	
ralmenis	**minerals**	
atts	**fats**	
ratew	**water**	
ttmnivas	**vitamins**	
droracbaytesh	**carbohydrates**	

Word Bank
proteins
vitamins
minerals
carbohydrates
water
fats

Nutrient Job Board
Match each nutrient from above with the job that it does for your body.

Needed: Nutrient to Deliver Food and Waste	Wanted: Muscle Builder and Body Repair Worker	Wanted: Nutrient to Store Energy
water	protein	fats

Needed: Quick Energy Supplier	Needed: Growth and Good Health Helper	Needed: Nutrients for Many Jobs, Including Building Strong Bones and Teeth
carbohydrates	vitamins	minerals

Find Out
How much of your body is water?

Page 42

The New "Big Four"

Name _____

Your body will get the nutrients it needs if you follow the rules of the food group pyramid. Be sure to make fruits, vegetables, and grains the basic foods of your diet. Eat plenty of healthy foods from the bottom of the pyramid every day.

oils, fats, sweets
eat very few

milk, yogurt, cheese – 2-3 servings daily

meat, fish, poultry, eggs, dry beans, nuts – 2-3 servings daily

fruits – 2-4 servings daily

vegetables – 3-5 servings daily

bread, cereal, pasta, rice – 6-11 servings each day

Find Out
What foods do you eat each day? Choose a day and make a chart of what you eat. Record the kind of food and the number of servings.

Group	Breakfast	Lunch	Dinner	Snack
Bread, cereal, pasta, rice				
Vegetables				
Fruits		Answers will vary.		
Meat, fish, poultry, eggs, dry beans, nuts				
milk, cheese, and yogurt				
Fats, oils, and sweets				

How did you do? Compare your servings with what is indicated on the food pyramid.

Page 43

Go Power

Name _____

Carbohydrates are the main source of quick energy. Foods with lots of sugar and starch are rich in carbohydrates. You get carbohydrates from many of your favorite foods like spaghetti, bread, cake, and candy.

Complete the sentences using words from the word bank.

Carbohydrates are the **first** foods to be digested.

Starches are changed to sugars.

Sugar gives us **energy**

Leftover sugar is stored as **fat**

Word Bank
fat
first
starches
energy

grains, peas, corn, potatoes, plums, apples

Fill in the plate with carbohydrate-rich foods. Find pictures of these foods in magazines, cut them out, and paste them on the plate.

Find Out
Sweet Test
1. Chew a soda cracker well. Keep it in your mouth for five minutes.
2. What is the new taste in your mouth?
3. What happened to the starch in the cracker?

Page 44

Energy Savers

Name _____

Fats give you twice as much energy as protein or carbohydrates. Your body uses fats to save energy for future use. The fats we eat come from animals in the form of meat, eggs, milk, and much more. We also get fats from some plants like beans, peanuts, and corn. But not all plants give us fats in our diet.

Look at the pictures.
Circle the foods which are rich in fat.
Then list them on the chart.

Fat Food Sources	
Animal	Plant
chicken	olive oil
cheese	corn (oil)
ice cream	margarine
red meat	peanuts
butter	legumes (beans)

Find Out

Here is a simple test to tell if a food has fat.
1. Cut a brown paper bag into several four-inch squares.
2. Rub a piece of food on a square until it looks wet.
3. Label the paper.
4. Let the paper dry overnight.
5. Hold the paper up to the window the next day. If there is a grease spot, the food contains fat.

Protein: The Body Builder

Name _____

Protein is the nutrient that repairs and builds new body tissue. Most of the foods we eat contain some protein. We call these "high protein foods."

Circle all of the high protein foods.

Did you notice that most of the foods you circled belong to two food groups? Name these groups and list the circled foods under the correct group. Add two more high protein foods to each list.

Group: **Meat and Protein**
1. fish
2. chicken
3. red meat
4. peanuts
5. hamburg
6. eggs

Group: **Dairy**
1. yogurt
2. cheese
3.
4.
5.
6.

Find Out

Legumes (dry peas and beans) are an important protein source in many countries around the world. List as many kinds of legumes as you can think of. (Hint: A trip to your favorite grocery store will help you answer this.)

Amazing "Vita-Men"

Name _____

Vitamins do many important jobs. They help us grow and stay healthy. We can get all of the vitamins we need by eating a well-balanced diet!

Guide the Vita-Men through the mazes to find out the jobs they do

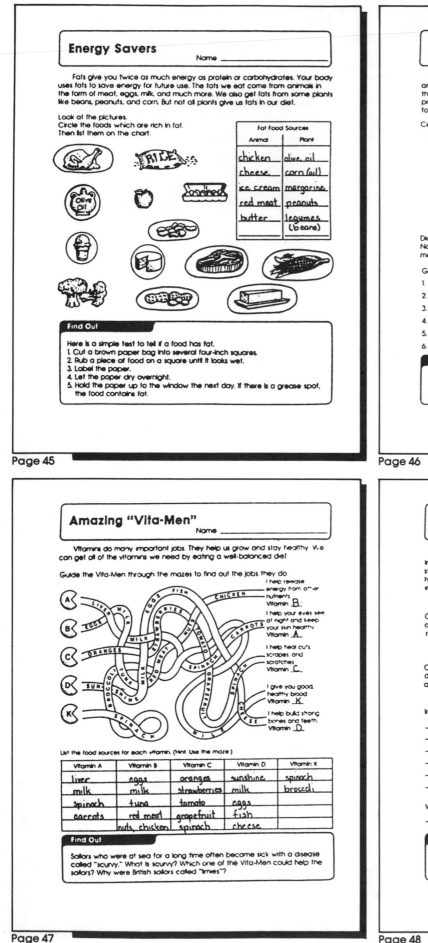

I help release energy from other nutrients. Vitamin **B**

I help your eyes see at night and keep your skin healthy. Vitamin **A**

I help heal cuts, scrapes, and scratches. Vitamin **C**

I give you good, healthy blood. Vitamin **K**

I help build strong bones and teeth. Vitamin **D**

List the food sources for each vitamin. (Hint: Use the maze.)

Vitamin A	Vitamin B	Vitamin C	Vitamin D	Vitamin K
liver	eggs	oranges	sunshine	spinach
milk	milk	strawberries	milk	broccoli
spinach	tuna	tomato	eggs	
carrots	red meat	grapefruit	fish	
	nuts, chicken	spinach	cheese	

Find Out

Sailors who were at sea for a long time often became sick with a disease called "scurvy." What is scurvy? Which one of the Vita-Men could help the sailors? Why were British sailors called "limes"?

Minerals

Name _____

Minerals like calcium and iron are very important nutrients. Calcium helps build strong bones and teeth. Iron helps build rich, healthy blood. Calcium and iron are found in many different kinds of food.

Circle the food words that are written across in the wordsearch. These foods are rich in iron. List them.

Circle the food words that are written up and down in the word search. These foods are rich in calcium. List them.

Iron-Rich Foods
beans
raisins
peas
clams
liver

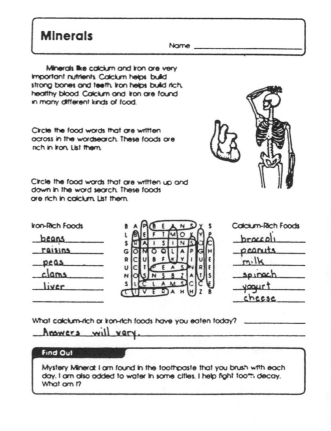

Calcium-Rich Foods
broccoli
peanuts
milk
spinach
yogurt
cheese

What calcium-rich or iron-rich foods have you eaten today? _____
Answers will vary.

Find Out

Mystery Mineral I am found in the toothpaste that you brush with each day. I am also added to water in some cities. I help fight tooth decay. What am I?

©1992 Instructional Fair, Inc.   114

Answer Key

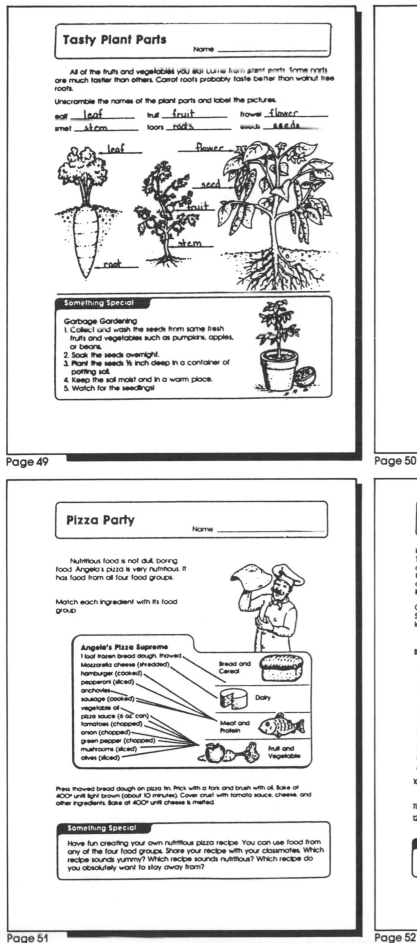

Page 49 — Tasty Plant Parts

Name _____

All of the fruits and vegetables you eat come from plant parts. Some parts are much tastier than others. Carrot roots probably taste better than walnut tree roots.

Unscramble the names of the plant parts and label the pictures.

eaf __leaf__   frull __fruit__   trowel __flower__
smet __stem__   toors __roots__   weeds __seeds__

Something Special

Garbage Gardening
1. Collect and wash the seeds from some fresh fruits and vegetables such as pumpkins, apples, or beans.
2. Soak the seeds overnight.
3. Plant the seeds ½ inch deep in a container of potting soil.
4. Keep the soil moist and in a warm place.
5. Watch for the seedlings!

Page 49

Page 50 — Vegetable Stand

Name _____

Help Leon sort all of his produce.
List the letter of each of the fruits and vegetables under the correct plant part.

Leon's Fresh Produce

A. celery   B. spinach   C. peanuts   D. asparagus   E. onion
F. carrots   G. broccoli   H. orange   I. radish   J. garlic
K. cabbage   L. apple   M. lettuce   N. peas   O. tomato

Stem	Leaf	Flower	Fruit	Seed	Root	Bulb
A	B	G	H	C	F	E
D	K		L		I	J
	M		N, N			
			O			

Fruity Vegetables   Circle the vegetables that are the fruits of the plant.

(pea pod)   cabbage   carrot   (string bean)
(cucumber)   (avocado)   broccoli   (green pepper)
spinach   (zucchini)   potato   turnip

Something Special

How many kinds of vegetables can you name? Write a list of as many vegetables as you can name. Circle the ones you like. Place an X in front of the ones you dislike. Place a ? in front of the ones you have never tasted.

Page 50

Page 51 — Pizza Party

Name _____

Nutritious food is not dull, boring food. Angelo's pizza is very nutritious. It has food from all four food groups.

Match each ingredient with its food group.

Angelo's Pizza Supreme
1 loaf frozen bread dough, thawed
Mozzarella cheese (shredded)
hamburger (cooked)
pepperoni (sliced)
anchovies
sausage (cooked)
vegetable oil
pizza sauce (6 oz. can)
tomatoes (chopped)
onion (chopped)
green pepper (chopped)
mushrooms (sliced)
olives (sliced)

Bread and Cereal
Dairy
Meat and Protein
Fruit and Vegetable

Press thawed bread dough on pizza tin. Prick with a fork and brush with oil. Bake at 400° until light brown (about 10 minutes). Cover crust with tomato sauce, cheese, and other ingredients. Bake at 400° until cheese is melted.

Something Special

Have fun creating your own nutritious pizza recipe. You can use food from any of the four food groups. Share your recipe with your classmates. Which recipe sounds yummy? Which recipe sounds nutritious? Which recipe do you absolutely want to stay away from?

Page 51

Page 52 — Labels

Name _____

Labels give us all kinds of information about the foods we eat. The ingredients of a food are listed in a special order. The ingredient with the largest amount is listed first, the one with the next largest amount is listed second, and so on.

Complete the "Breakfast Table Label Survey" using information from the label on this page.

Breakfast Table Label Survey

1. What does R.D.A. mean? __Recommended Daily Allowances__
2. Calories per serving with milk __190__
3. Calories per serving without milk __110__
4. Calories per ½ cup serving of milk __80__
5. Protein per serving with milk __5 g__
6. Protein per serving without milk __1 g__
7. Protein in ½ cup serving of milk __4 g__
8. Percentage U.S. R.D.A. of Vitamin C __0__
9. First ingredient __corn flour__
10. Is sugar a listed ingredient? __yes__
    If yes, in what place is it listed? __second__
11. Were any vitamins added? __yes__
12. What preservative was added? __BHA__

Find Out

What food product has this ingredient label?
"Carbonated water, sugar, corn sweetener, natural flavorings, caramel color, phosphoric acid, caffeine."

Page 52

Answer Key

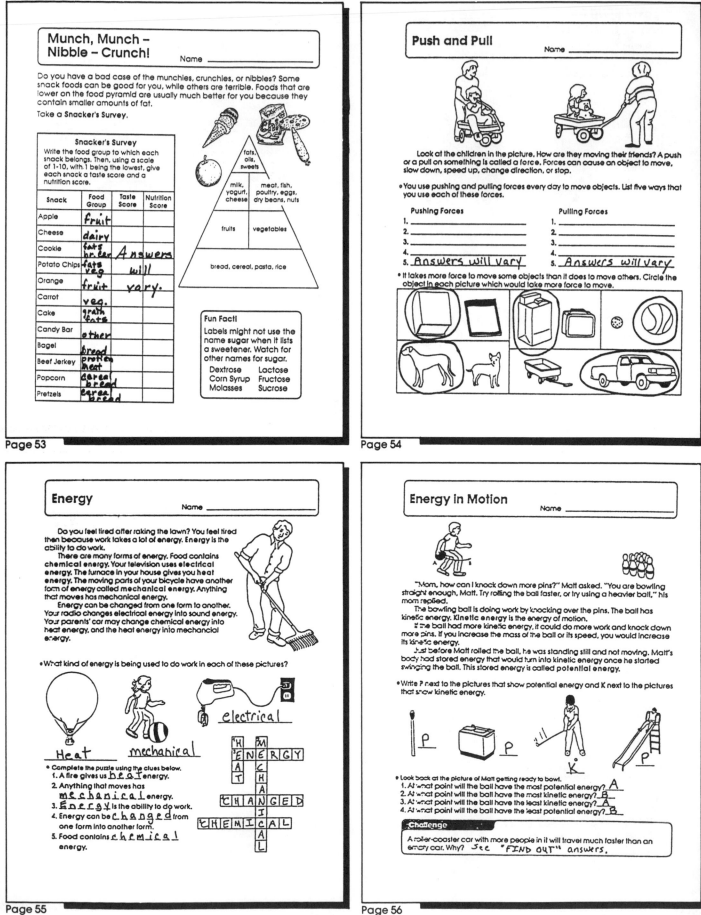

Munch, Munch – Nibble – Crunch!
Name _____

Do you have a bad case of the munchies, crunchies, or nibbles? Some snack foods can be good for you, while others are terrible. Foods that are lower on the food pyramid are usually much better for you because they contain smaller amounts of fat.

Take a Snacker's Survey.

Snacker's Survey
Write the food group to which each snack belongs. Then, using a scale of 1-10, with 1 being the lowest, give each snack a taste score and a nutrition score.

Snack	Food Group	Taste Score	Nutrition Score
Apple	fruit		
Cheese	dairy		
Cookie	fats br. cer		
Potato Chips	fats veg		
Orange	fruit		
Carrot	veg.		
Cake	grain fats		
Candy Bar	other		
Bagel	bread		
Beef Jerky	protein meat		
Popcorn	cereal bread		
Pretzels	cereal bread		

Answers will vary.

Food pyramid:
- fats, oils, sweets
- milk, yogurt, cheese
- meat, fish, poultry, eggs, dry beans, nuts
- fruits
- vegetables
- bread, cereal, pasta, rice

Fun Fact!
Labels might not use the name **sugar** when it lists a sweetener. Watch for other names for sugar.

Dextrose	Lactose
Corn Syrup	Fructose
Molasses	Sucrose

Page 53

Push and Pull
Name _____

Look at the children in the picture. How are they moving their friends? A push or a pull on something is called a force. Forces can cause an object to move, slow down, speed up, change direction, or stop.

• You use pushing and pulling forces every day to move objects. List five ways that you use each of these forces.

Pushing Forces
1. _____
2. _____
3. _____
4. _____
5. _Answers will vary_

Pulling Forces
1. _____
2. _____
3. _____
4. _____
5. _Answers will vary_

• It takes more force to move some objects than it does to move others. Circle the object in each picture which would take more force to move.

Page 54

Energy
Name _____

Do you feel tired after raking the lawn? You feel tired then because work takes a lot of energy. Energy is the ability to do work.

There are many forms of energy. Food contains chemical energy. Your television uses electrical energy. The furnace in your house gives you heat energy. The moving parts of your bicycle have another form of energy called mechanical energy. Anything that moves has mechanical energy.

Energy can be changed from one form to another. Your radio changes electrical energy into sound energy. Your parents' car may change chemical energy into heat energy, and the heat energy into mechanical energy.

• What kind of energy is being used to do work in each of these pictures?

Heat   mechanical   electrical

• Complete the puzzle using the clues below.
1. A fire gives us h e a t energy.
2. Anything that moves has m e c h a n i c a l energy.
3. E n e r g y is the ability to do work.
4. Energy can be c h a n g e d from one form into another form.
5. Food contains c h e m i c a l energy.

Page 55

Energy in Motion
Name _____

"Mom, how can I knock down more pins?" Matt asked. "You are bowling straight enough, Matt. Try rolling the ball faster, or try using a heavier ball," his mom replied.

The bowling ball is doing work by knocking over the pins. The ball has kinetic energy. Kinetic energy is the energy of motion.

If the ball had more kinetic energy, it could do more work and knock down more pins. If you increase the mass of the ball or its speed, you would increase its kinetic energy.

Just before Matt rolled the ball, he was standing still and not moving. Matt's body had stored energy that would turn into kinetic energy once he started swinging the ball. This stored energy is called potential energy.

• Write P next to the pictures that show potential energy and K next to the pictures that show kinetic energy.

P   P   K   P

• Look back at the picture of Matt getting ready to bowl.
1. At what point will the ball have the most potential energy? A
2. At what point will the ball have the most kinetic energy? B
3. At what point will the ball have the least kinetic energy? A
4. At what point will the ball have the least potential energy? B

Challenge
A roller-coaster car with more people in it will travel much faster than an empty car. Why? See "FIND OUT" answers.

Page 56

©1992 Instructional Fair, Inc.

IF8758 Science Enrichment

Answer Key

Ramps, Hills, and Slopes
Name _____

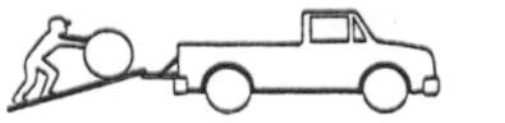

Word Bank	
machine	easier
force	inclined
shorter	longer

- Fill in the blanks with words from the Word Bank.

  Simple machines help people do work. In the picture above, the ramp makes the man's work a lot **easier**. The ramp is a simple **machine** called an inclined plane.

  An **inclined** plane makes work easier. It lessens the amount of force needed to move a load. By using the ramp, the man moves the barrel with much less force than if he tried to lift the barrel himself. With the ramp, the man moves the barrel a **longer** distance, but with much less force. By just lifting the barrel onto the truck, he would move it a **shorter** distance, but would need to use much more **force**.

- Ramps are used in many places to help people in wheelchairs get around more easily. List some places where ramps are used in your community.

  1. _____
  2. **Answers will vary.**
  3. _____

  The angle of an inclined plane affects the amount of force needed to lift an object. The longer and less steep the inclined plane is, the less force it takes to lift an object.

- Study the pictures below and then answer the questions.

  1. On which ramp will the barrel have to travel the farthest to get on the truck? **A**
  2. On which ramp will the least amount of force be needed to roll the barrel onto the truck? **A**
  3. How does the angle of the ramp affect the force needed to move the barrel? **The steeper the angle, the more force is needed.**

Find Out
How did the early Egyptians use inclined planes to build the great pyramids? **See "Find Out" answers.**

Page 57

Special Inclined Planes
Name _____

"Poof!" Leroy just shrank himself again in his "Super Electric Shrinking Machine." He is trying to decide which would be easier—climbing around and around the threads of a screw to get to the top or just climbing straight up the side of the screw. He found that the distance up the winding ramp is a lot farther, but the traveling is much easier than going straight up the side. The winding ramp of the screw is like a spiral stairway.

- Answer these questions.
  1. Would you travel a farther distance climbing a spiral stairway up three floors or climbing a ladder straight up three floors? **the stairway would be farther**
  2. Which would take more force to climb—the stairway or the ladder? **the ladder would take more force**
  3. When you climb a spiral stairway, you travel a greater **DISTANCE** but you use less **FORCE**.

  A screw is a special kind of inclined plane. A spiral stairway is also an inclined plane.

  Two or more inclined planes that are joined together to make a sharp edge or point form a wedge. A wedge is a special kind of inclined plane. A wedge is used to pierce or split things. A knife is a wedge. Can you name some other wedges?

- Some special inclined planes are pictured below. Label each picture either a wedge or a screw.

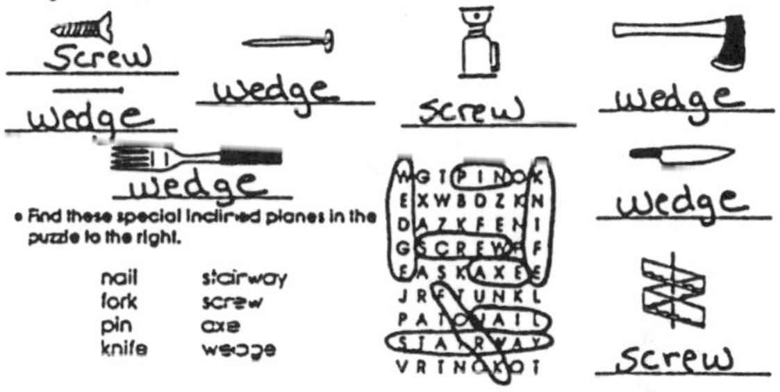

  Screw   **wedge**   **screw**   **wedge**

  wedge   **wedge**   **wedge**   **screw**

- Find these special inclined planes in the puzzle to the right.

nail	stairway
fork	screw
pin	axe
knife	wedge

  W G T P I N K
  E X W B D Z K
  D A Z K F E N I
  G S C R E W F
  E A S K A X E
  J R F U N K L
  P A I O N A I L
  S T A I R W A Y
  V R T N O X O T

Page 58

Levers
Name _____

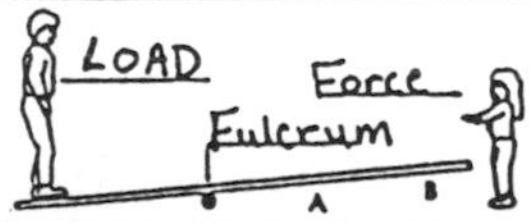

Word Bank	
simple	force
easier	load
fulcrum	distance
A	B

LOAD   Force   Fulcrum

- Use the words from the Word Bank to complete the sentences.

  Mandy wants to try to lift her dad off the ground. Where should Mandy stand on the board? By standing on point **B**, Mandy can lift her dad.

  The board resting on the log is an example of a **simple** machine called a lever. A lever has three parts—the force, the fulcrum, and the load. Mandy is the force. The point on which the lever turns is called the **fulcrum**. And Mandy's dad, the object to be lifted, is called the **load**. The greater the **distance** between the **force** and the fulcrum, the **easier** it is to lift the load. The closer the distance between the force and the fulcrum, the harder it is to lift the load.

- Label the picture of Mandy and her father with these words: load, force, and fulcrum.

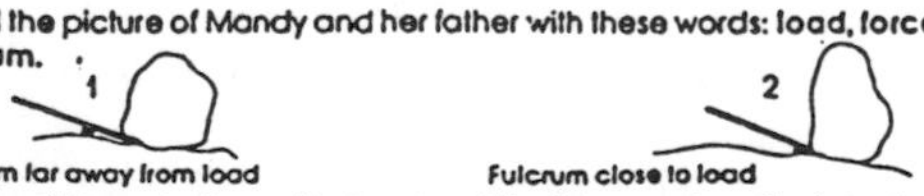

  1. Fulcrum far away from load
  2. Fulcrum close to load

  The distance between the load and the fulcrum also affects the force needed to lift a load. The closer the fulcrum is to the load, the easier it is to lift the load.

- Look at the pictures above to answer these questions.
  1. Matt wants to move a large rock with a lever. Which lever would let him use the least amount of force to move the rock? **2**
  2. Which lever would have to be moved the greatest distance to move the rock? **2**
  3. Why is a lever called a simple machine? **Simple machines make work easier by letting you use less force.**

- Label the force, fulcrum, and load of the levers below.

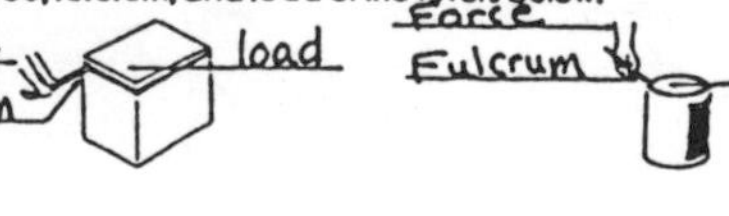

  Force   Fulcrum   load   Force   Fulcrum   load

Page 59

Around and Around
Name _____

A doorknob is a simple machine you use every day. It is a wheel and axle machine. The wheel is connected to the axle. The axle is a center post. When the wheel moves, the axle does too.

Opening a door by turning the axle with your fingers is very hard. But by turning the doorknob, which is the "wheel," you use much less force. The doorknob turns the axle for you. The doorknob makes it easy because it is much bigger than the axle. You turn the doorknob a greater distance, but with much less force.

Sometimes the "wheel" of a wheel and axle machine doesn't look like a wheel. But look at the path the doorknob, a wheel, makes when it is turned. The path makes a circle, just like a wheel.

- Color just the wheels of the wheel and axle machines below.

- Look at the pictures to the right and answer these questions.
  1. A screwdriver is a wheel and axle. What part of a screwdriver is the wheel? **the handle** 
  2. What part of a screwdriver is the axle? **the stem**
  3. Which screwdriver to the right has the largest wheel? **B**
  4. Which screwdriver would take the least amount of force to turn? **B**
  5. Which screwdriver must travel the greatest distance? **B**

Stumper
Why is the crank on a meat grinder larger than the crank on a pencil sharpener?
Why is the steering wheel on a truck larger than the steering wheel on a car? **SEE "FIND OUT" ANSWERS.**

Page 60

Answer Key

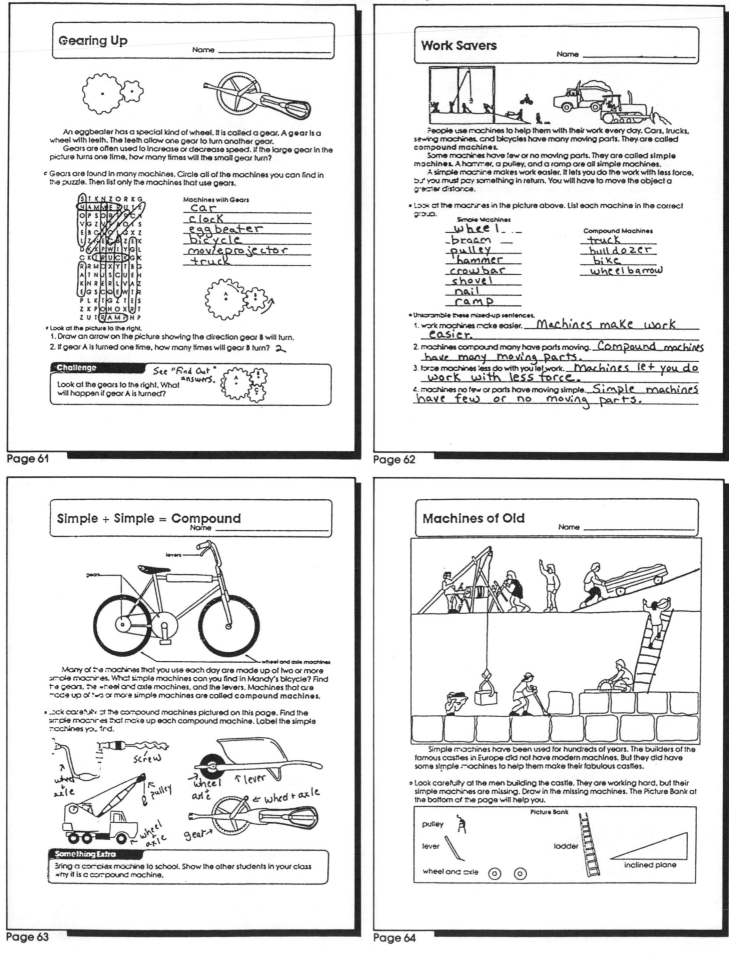

Gearing Up

Name _____

An eggbeater has a special kind of wheel. It is called a gear. A gear is a wheel with teeth. The teeth allow one gear to turn another gear.

Gears are often used to increase or decrease speed. If the large gear in the picture turns one time, how many times will the small gear turn?

• Gears are found in many machines. Circle all of the machines you can find in the puzzle. Then list only the machines that use gears.

```
S I K N Z O R K G
H A M M E R U T A
O P S O R R C L I
V G Z M V R O S X
E B C C G X C G X Z
L Z P Z E Z E X
D E X P W I Y G L
C K T R U C K G K
R R M E X Y T B G
A T N J S C U E H
K N R E R L V A Z
E G S C O L E W T R
P L K T G Z T E S
Z K P O H O X R T
Z U T R A M P N P
```

Machines with Gears
car
clock
eggbeater
bicycle
movie projector
truck

• Look at the picture to the right.
1. Draw an arrow on the picture showing the direction gear B will turn.
2. If gear A is turned one time, how many times will gear B turn? **2**

Challenge
Look at the gears to the right. What will happen if gear A is turned?
See "Find Out" answers.

Page 61

Work Savers

Name _____

People use machines to help them with their work every day. Cars, trucks, sewing machines, and bicycles have many moving parts. They are called compound machines.

Some machines have few or no moving parts. They are called simple machines. A hammer, a pulley, and a ramp are all simple machines.

A simple machine makes work easier. It lets you do the work with less force, but you must pay something in return. You will have to move the object a greater distance.

• Look at the machines in the picture above. List each machine in the correct group.

Simple Machines
wheel
broom
pulley
hammer
crowbar
shovel
nail
ramp

Compound Machines
truck
bulldozer
bike
wheelbarrow

• Unscramble these mixed-up sentences.
1. work machines make easier. **Machines make work easier.**
2. machines compound many have parts moving. **Compound machines have many moving parts.**
3. force machines less do with you let work. **Machines let you do work with less force.**
4. machines no few or parts have moving simple. **Simple machines have few or no moving parts.**

Page 62

Simple + Simple = Compound

Name _____

Many of the machines that you use each day are made up of two or more simple machines. What simple machines can you find in Mandy's bicycle? Find the gears, the wheel and axle machines, and the levers. Machines that are made up of two or more simple machines are called compound machines.

• Look carefully at the compound machines pictured on this page. Find the simple machines that make up each compound machine. Label the simple machines you find.

screw
wheel axle
pulley
wheel axle
wheel axle
lever
wheel + axle
gear

Something Extra
Bring a complex machine to school. Show the other students in your class why it is a compound machine.

Page 63

Machines of Old

Name _____

Simple machines have been used for hundreds of years. The builders of the famous castles in Europe did not have modern machines. But they did have some simple machines to help them make their fabulous castles.

• Look carefully at the men building the castle. They are working hard, but their simple machines are missing. Draw in the missing machines. The Picture Bank at the bottom of the page will help you.

Picture Bank
pulley
lever
wheel and axle
ladder
inclined plane

Page 64

©1992 Instructional Fair, Inc.

IF8758 Science Enrichment

Answer Key

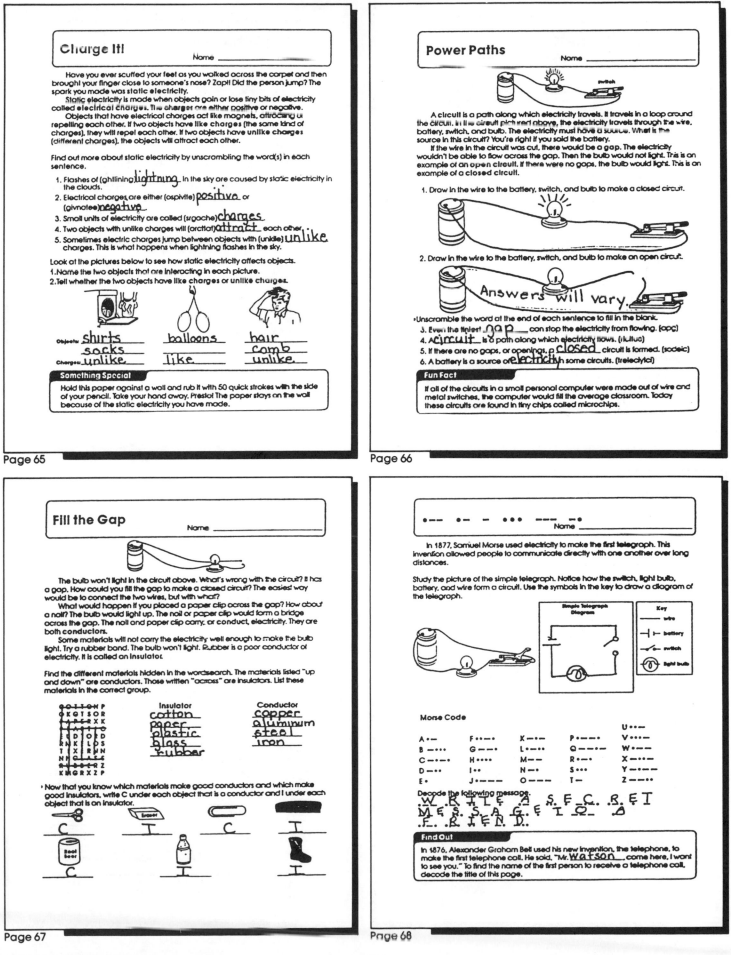

Charge It!

Name _____

Have you ever scuffed your feet as you walked across the carpet and then brought your finger close to someone's nose? Zap!! Did the person jump? The spark you made was static electricity.

Static electricity is made when objects gain or lose tiny bits of electricity called electrical charges. The charges are either positive or negative.

Objects that have electrical charges act like magnets, attracting or repelling each other. If two objects have like charges (the same kind of charges), they will repel each other. If two objects have unlike charges (different charges), the objects will attract each other.

Find out more about static electricity by unscrambling the word(s) in each sentence.

1. Flashes of (ghtinling) **lightning** in the sky are caused by static electricity in the clouds.
2. Electrical charges are either (ospivite) **positive** or (givnotee) **negative**.
3. Small units of electricity are called (srgoache) **charges**.
4. Two objects with unlike charges will (arcttat) **attract** each other.
5. Sometimes electric charges jump between objects with (unlide) **unlike** charges. This is what happens when lightning flashes in the sky.

Look at the pictures below to see how static electricity affects objects.
1. Name the two objects that are interacting in each picture.
2. Tell whether the two objects have like charges or unlike charges.

Objects: **shirts socks** / **balloons** / **hair comb**
Charges: **unlike** / **like** / **unlike**

Something Special
Hold this paper against a wall and rub it with 50 quick strokes with the side of your pencil. Take your hand away. Presto! The paper stays on the wall because of the static electricity you have made.

Page 65

Power Paths

Name _____

A circuit is a path along which electricity travels. It travels in a loop around the circuit. In the circuit pictured above, the electricity travels through the wire, battery, switch, and bulb. The electricity must have a source. What is the source in this circuit? You're right if you said the battery.

If the wire in the circuit was cut, there would be a gap. The electricity wouldn't be able to flow across the gap. Then the bulb would not light. This is an example of an open circuit. If there were no gaps, the bulb would light. This is an example of a closed circuit.

1. Draw in the wire to the battery, switch, and bulb to make a closed circuit.

2. Draw in the wire to the battery, switch, and bulb to make an open circuit.

Answers will vary.

•Unscramble the word at the end of each sentence to fill in the blank.
3. Even the tiniest **gap** can stop the electricity from flowing. (apg)
4. A **circuit** is a path along which electricity flows. (ritiuc)
5. If there are no gaps, or openings, a **closed** circuit is formed. (sodeic)
6. A battery is a source of **electricity** in some circuits. (treleciytci)

Fun Fact
If all of the circuits in a small personal computer were made out of wire and metal switches, the computer would fill the average classroom. Today these circuits are found in tiny chips called microchips.

Page 66

Fill the Gap

Name _____

The bulb won't light in the circuit above. What's wrong with the circuit? It has a gap. How could you fill the gap to make a closed circuit? The easiest way would be to connect the two wires, but with what?

What would happen if you placed a paper clip across the gap? How about a nail? The bulb would light up. The nail or paper clip would form a bridge across the gap. The nail and paper clip carry, or conduct, electricity. They are both conductors.

Some materials will not carry the electricity well enough to make the bulb light. Try a rubber band. The bulb won't light. Rubber is a poor conductor of electricity. It is called an insulator.

Find the different materials hidden in the wordsearch. The materials listed "up and down" are conductors. Those written "across" are insulators. List these materials in the correct group.

Insulator	Conductor
cotton	copper
paper	aluminum
plastic	steel
glass	iron
rubber	

•Now that you know which materials make good conductors and which make good insulators, write C under each object that is a conductor and I under each object that is an insulator.

C / I / C / I
C / I / C

Page 67

· — ·   · — ·   —   · · ·   — — —   — •
Name _____

In 1877, Samuel Morse used electricity to make the first telegraph. This invention allowed people to communicate directly with one another over long distances.

Study the picture of the simple telegraph. Notice how the switch, light bulb, battery, and wire form a circuit. Use the symbols in the key to draw a diagram of the telegraph.

Morse Code

A ·—	F ··—·	K —·—	P ·——·	U ··—
B —···	G ——·	L ·—··	Q ——·—	V ···—
C —·—·	H ····	M ——	R ·—·	W ·——
D —··	I ··	N —·	S ···	X —··—
E ·	J ·———	O ———	T —	Y —·——
				Z ——··

Decode the following message.
WRITE A SECRET MESSAGE TO A FRIEND.

Find Out
In 1876, Alexander Graham Bell used his new invention, the telephone, to make the first telephone call. He said, "Mr. **Watson** come here, I want to see you." To find the name of the first person to receive a telephone call, decode the title of this page.

Page 68

Answer Key

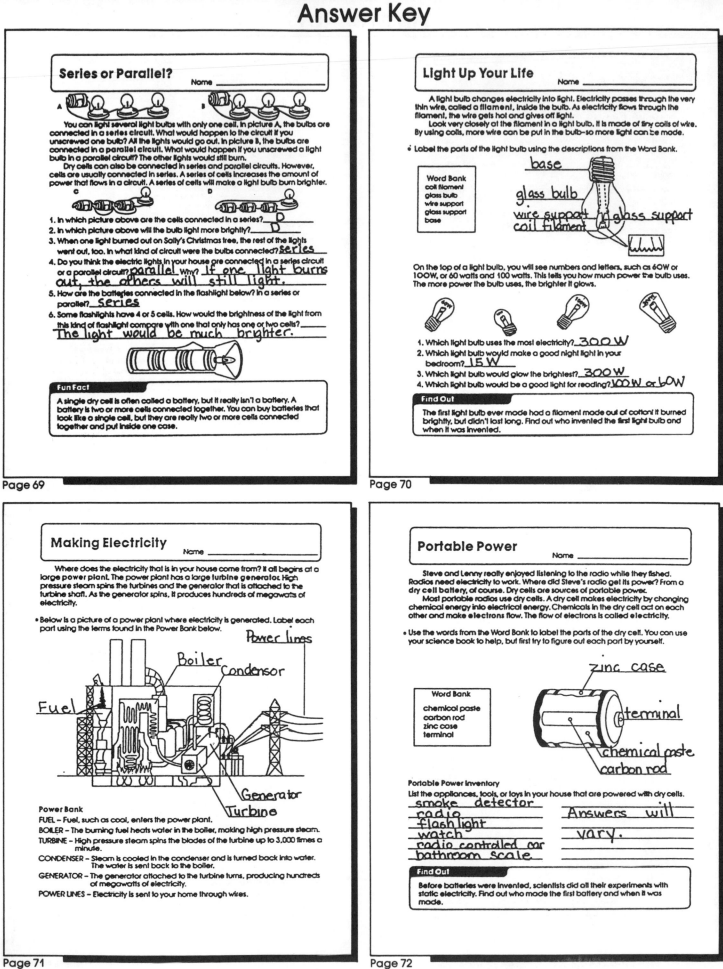

Series or Parallel?

Name _____

You can light several light bulbs with only one cell. In picture A, the bulbs are connected in a series circuit. What would happen to the circuit if you unscrewed one bulb? All the lights would go out. In picture B, the bulbs are connected in a parallel circuit. What would happen if you unscrewed a light bulb in a parallel circuit? The other lights would still burn.

Dry cells can also be connected in series and parallel circuits. However, cells are usually connected in series. A series of cells increases the amount of power that flows in a circuit. A series of cells will make a light bulb burn brighter.

1. In which picture above are the cells connected in a series? C
2. In which picture above will the bulb light more brightly? D
3. When one light burned out on Sally's Christmas tree, the rest of the lights went out, too. In what kind of circuit were the bulbs connected? series
4. Do you think the electric lights in your house are connected in a series circuit or a parallel circuit? parallel Why? If one light burns out, the others will still light.
5. How are the batteries connected in the flashlight below? In a series or parallel? series
6. Some flashlights have 4 or 5 cells. How would the brightness of the light from this kind of flashlight compare with one that only has one or two cells? The light would be much brighter.

Fun Fact
A single dry cell is often called a battery, but it really isn't a battery. A battery is two or more cells connected together. You can buy batteries that look like a single cell, but they are really two or more cells connected together and put inside one case.

Page 69

Light Up Your Life

Name _____

A light bulb changes electricity into light. Electricity passes through the very thin wire, called a filament, inside the bulb. As electricity flows through the filament, the wire gets hot and gives off light.

Look very closely at the filament in a light bulb. It is made of tiny coils of wire. By using coils, more wire can be put in the bulb–so more light can be made.

• Label the parts of the light bulb using the descriptions from the Word Bank.

Word Bank
coil filament
glass bulb
wire support
glass support
base

base
glass bulb
wire support / glass support
coil filament

On the top of a light bulb, you will see numbers and letters, such as 60W or 100W, or 60 watts and 100 watts. This tells you how much power the bulb uses. The more power the bulb uses, the brighter it glows.

1. Which light bulb uses the most electricity? 300 W
2. Which light bulb would make a good night light in your bedroom? 15 W
3. Which light bulb would glow the brightest? 300 W
4. Which light bulb would be a good light for reading? 100 W or 60W

Find Out
The first light bulb ever made had a filament made out of cotton! It burned brightly, but didn't last long. Find out who invented the first light bulb and when it was invented.

Page 70

Making Electricity

Name _____

Where does the electricity that is in your house come from? It all begins at a large power plant. The power plant has a large turbine generator. High pressure steam spins the turbines and the generator that is attached to the turbine shaft. As the generator spins, it produces hundreds of megawatts of electricity.

• Below is a picture of a power plant where electricity is generated. Label each part using the terms found in the Power Bank below.

Power lines
Boiler
Condensor
Fuel
Generator
Turbine

Power Bank
FUEL – Fuel, such as coal, enters the power plant.
BOILER – The burning fuel heats water in the boiler, making high pressure steam.
TURBINE – High pressure steam spins the blades of the turbine up to 3,000 times a minute.
CONDENSER – Steam is cooled in the condenser and is turned back into water. The water is sent back to the boiler.
GENERATOR – The generator attached to the turbine turns, producing hundreds of megawatts of electricity.
POWER LINES – Electricity is sent to your home through wires.

Page 71

Portable Power

Name _____

Steve and Lenny really enjoyed listening to the radio while they fished. Radios need electricity to work. Where did Steve's radio get its power? From a dry cell battery, of course. Dry cells are sources of portable power.

Most portable radios use dry cells. A dry cell makes electricity by changing chemical energy into electrical energy. Chemicals in the dry cell act on each other and make electrons flow. The flow of electrons is called electricity.

• Use the words from the Word Bank to label the parts of the dry cell. You can use your science book to help, but first try to figure out each part by yourself.

Word Bank
chemical paste
carbon rod
zinc case
terminal

zinc case
terminal
chemical paste
carbon rod

Portable Power Inventory
List the appliances, tools, or toys in your house that are powered with dry cells.
smoke detector
radio
flashlight
watch
radio controlled car
bathroom scale
Answers will vary.

Find Out
Before batteries were invented, scientists did all their experiments with static electricity. Find out who made the first battery and when it was made.

Page 72

Answer Key

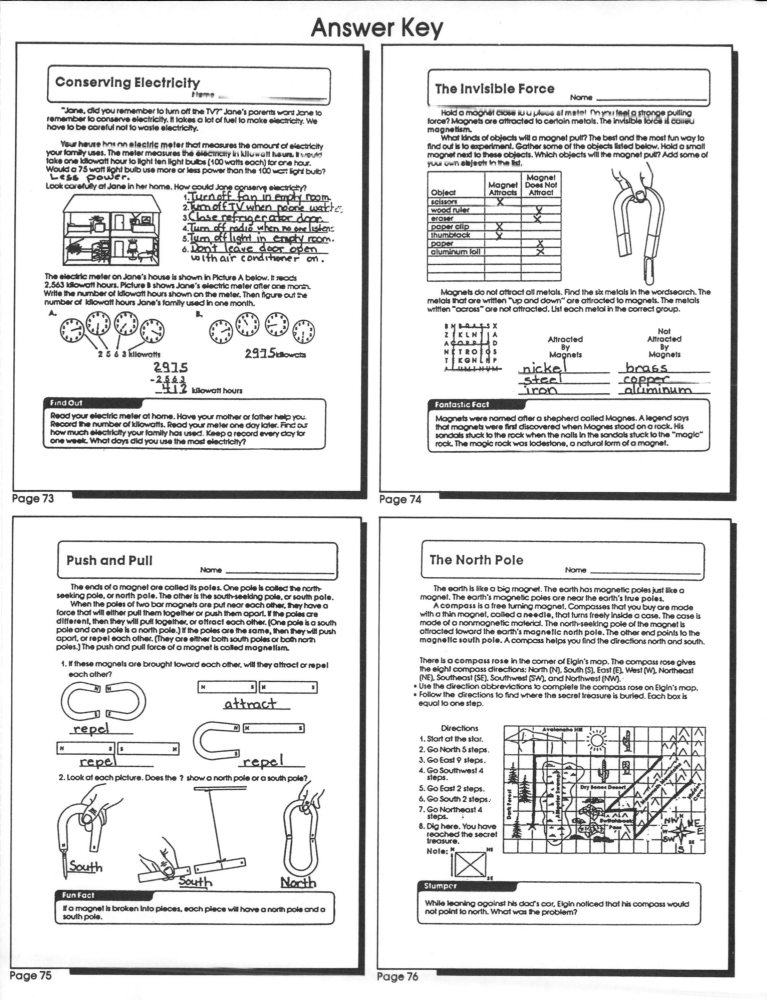

Conserving Electricity

Name _____

"Jane, did you remember to turn off the TV?" Jane's parents want Jane to remember to conserve electricity. It takes a lot of fuel to make electricity. We have to be careful not to waste electricity.

Your house has an electric meter that measures the amount of electricity your family uses. The meter measures the electricity in kilowatt hours. It would take one kilowatt hour to light ten light bulbs (100 watts each) for one hour. Would a 75 watt light bulb use more or less power than the 100 watt light bulb? **Less power.**
Look carefully at Jane in her home. How could Jane conserve electricity?

1. Turn off fan in empty room.
2. Turn off TV when no one watches.
3. Close refrigerator door.
4. Turn off radio when no one listens.
5. Turn off light in empty room.
6. Don't leave door open with air conditioner on.

The electric meter on Jane's house is shown in Picture A below. It reads 2,563 kilowatt hours. Picture B shows Jane's electric meter after one month. Write the number of kilowatt hours shown on the meter. Then figure out the number of kilowatt hours Jane's family used in one month.

A. 2 5 6 3 kilowatts

B. 2975 kilowatts

$$2975$$
$$-2563$$
$$\overline{412} \text{ kilowatt hours}$$

Find Out

Read your electric meter at home. Have your mother or father help you. Record the number of kilowatts. Read your meter one day later. Find out how much electricity your family has used. Keep a record every day for one week. What days did you use the most electricity?

The Invisible Force

Name _____

Hold a magnet close to a piece of metal. Do you feel a strong pulling force? Magnets are attracted to certain metals. The invisible force is called magnetism.
What kinds of objects will a magnet pull? The best and the most fun way to find out is to experiment. Gather some of the objects listed below. Hold a small magnet next to these objects. Which objects will the magnet pull? Add some of your own objects to the list.

Object	Magnet Attracts	Magnet Does Not Attract
scissors	X	
wood ruler		X
eraser		X
paper clip	X	
thumbtack	X	
paper		X
aluminum foil		X

Magnets do not attract all metals. Find the six metals in the wordsearch. The metals that are written "up and down" are attracted to magnets. The metals written "across" are not attracted. List each metal in the correct group.

B	M	B	R	A	S	S	X
Z	K	L	N	T	I	A	
A	C	O	P	P	E	R	D
N	C	T	R	O	I	Q	S
T	Y	K	G	N	L	N	P
A	L	U	M	I	N	U	M

Attracted By Magnets
nickel
steel
iron

Not Attracted By Magnets
brass
copper
aluminum

Fantastic Fact

Magnets were named after a shepherd called Magnes. A legend says that magnets were first discovered when Magnes stood on a rock. His sandals stuck to the rock when the nails in the sandals stuck to the "magic" rock. The magic rock was lodestone, a natural form of a magnet.

Push and Pull

Name _____

The ends of a magnet are called its poles. One pole is called the north-seeking pole, or north pole. The other is the south-seeking pole, or south pole.
When the poles of two bar magnets are put near each other, they have a force that will either pull them together or push them apart. If the poles are different, then they will pull together, or attract each other. (One pole is a south pole and one pole is a north pole.) If the poles are the same, then they will push apart, or repel each other. (They are either both south poles or both north poles.) The push and pull force of a magnet is called magnetism.

1. If these magnets are brought toward each other, will they attract or repel each other?

attract

repel

repel

repel

2. Look at each picture. Does the ? show a north pole or a south pole?

South

South

North

Fun Fact

If a magnet is broken into pieces, each piece will have a north pole and a south pole.

The North Pole

Name _____

The earth is like a big magnet. The earth has magnetic poles just like a magnet. The earth's magnetic poles are near the earth's true poles.
A compass is a free turning magnet. Compasses that you buy are made with a thin magnet, called a needle, that turns freely inside a case. The case is made of a nonmagnetic material. The north-seeking pole of the magnet is attracted toward the earth's magnetic north pole. The other end points to the magnetic south pole. A compass helps you find the directions north and south.

There is a compass rose in the corner of Elgin's map. The compass rose gives the eight compass directions: North (N), South (S), East (E), West (W), Northeast (NE), Southeast (SE), Southwest (SW), and Northwest (NW).
• Use the direction abbreviations to complete the compass rose on Elgin's map.
• Follow the directions to find where the secret treasure is buried. Each box is equal to one step.

Directions
1. Start at the star.
2. Go North 5 steps.
3. Go East 9 steps.
4. Go Southwest 4 steps.
5. Go East 2 steps.
6. Go South 2 steps.
7. Go Northeast 4 steps.
8. Dig here. You have reached the secret treasure.

Note:

Stumper

While leaning against his dad's car, Elgin noticed that his compass would not point to north. What was the problem?

©1992 Instructional Fair, Inc.   121   IF8758 Science Enrichment

Answer Key

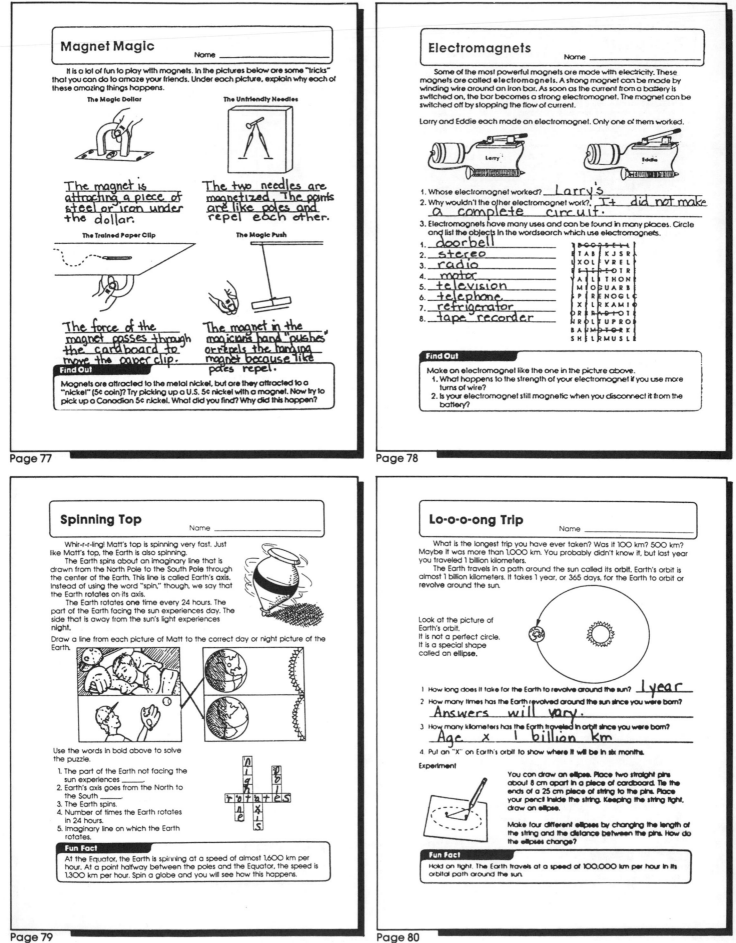

Magnet Magic

Name _____

It is a lot of fun to play with magnets. In the pictures below are some "tricks" that you can do to amaze your friends. Under each picture, explain why each of these amazing things happens.

The Magic Dollar

The magnet is attracting a piece of steel or iron under the dollar.

The Unfriendly Needles

The two needles are magnetized. The points are like poles and repel each other.

The Trained Paper Clip

The force of the magnet passes through the cardboard to move the paper clip.

The Magic Push

The magnet in the magician's hand "pushes" or repels the hanging magnet because like poles repel.

Find Out

Magnets are attracted to the metal nickel, but are they attracted to a "nickel" (5¢ coin)? Try picking up a U.S. 5¢ nickel with a magnet. Now try to pick up a Canadian 5¢ nickel. What did you find? Why did this happen?

Page 77

Electromagnets

Name _____

Some of the most powerful magnets are made with electricity. These magnets are called electromagnets. A strong magnet can be made by winding wire around an iron bar. As soon as the current from a battery is switched on, the bar becomes a strong electromagnet. The magnet can be switched off by stopping the flow of current.

Larry and Eddie each made an electromagnet. Only one of them worked.

1. Whose electromagnet worked? __Larry's__
2. Why wouldn't the other electromagnet work? __It did not make a complete circuit.__
3. Electromagnets have many uses and can be found in many places. Circle and list the objects in the wordsearch which use electromagnets.

1. doorbell
2. stereo
3. radio
4. motor
5. television
6. telephone
7. refrigerator
8. tape recorder

Find Out

Make an electromagnet like the one in the picture above.
1. What happens to the strength of your electromagnet if you use more turns of wire?
2. Is your electromagnet still magnetic when you disconnect it from the battery?

Page 78

Spinning Top

Name _____

Whir-r-r-ling! Matt's top is spinning very fast. Just like Matt's top, the Earth is also spinning.

The Earth spins about an imaginary line that is drawn from the North Pole to the South Pole through the center of the Earth. This line is called Earth's **axis**. Instead of using the word "spin," though, we say that the Earth **rotates** on its axis.

The Earth rotates one time every 24 hours. The part of the Earth facing the sun experiences day. The side that is away from the sun's light experiences night.

Draw a line from each picture of Matt to the correct day or night picture of the Earth.

Use the words in bold above to solve the puzzle.

1. The part of the Earth not facing the sun experiences _____.
2. Earth's axis goes from the North to the South _____.
3. The Earth spins.
4. Number of times the Earth rotates in 24 hours.
5. Imaginary line on which the Earth rotates.

Fun Fact

At the Equator, the Earth is spinning at a speed of almost 1,600 km per hour. At a point halfway between the poles and the Equator, the speed is 1,300 km per hour. Spin a globe and you will see how this happens.

Page 79

Lo-o-o-ong Trip

Name _____

What is the longest trip you have ever taken? Was it 100 km? 500 km? Maybe it was more than 1,000 km. You probably didn't know it, but last year you traveled 1 billion kilometers.

The Earth travels in a path around the sun called its orbit. Earth's orbit is almost 1 billion kilometers. It takes 1 year, or 365 days, for the Earth to orbit or revolve around the sun.

Look at the picture of Earth's orbit. It is not a perfect circle. It is a special shape called an ellipse.

1. How long does it take for the Earth to revolve around the sun? __1 year__
2. How many times has the Earth revolved around the sun since you were born? __Answers will vary.__
3. How many kilometers has the Earth traveled in orbit since you were born? __Age x 1 billion km__
4. Put an "X" on Earth's orbit to show where it will be in six months.

Experiment

You can draw an ellipse. Place two straight pins about 8 cm apart in a piece of cardboard. Tie the ends of a 25 cm piece of string to the pins. Place your pencil inside the string. Keeping the string tight, draw an ellipse.

Make four different ellipses by changing the length of the string and the distance between the pins. How do the ellipses change?

Fun Fact

Hold on tight. The Earth travels at a speed of 100,000 km per hour in its orbital path around the sun.

Page 80

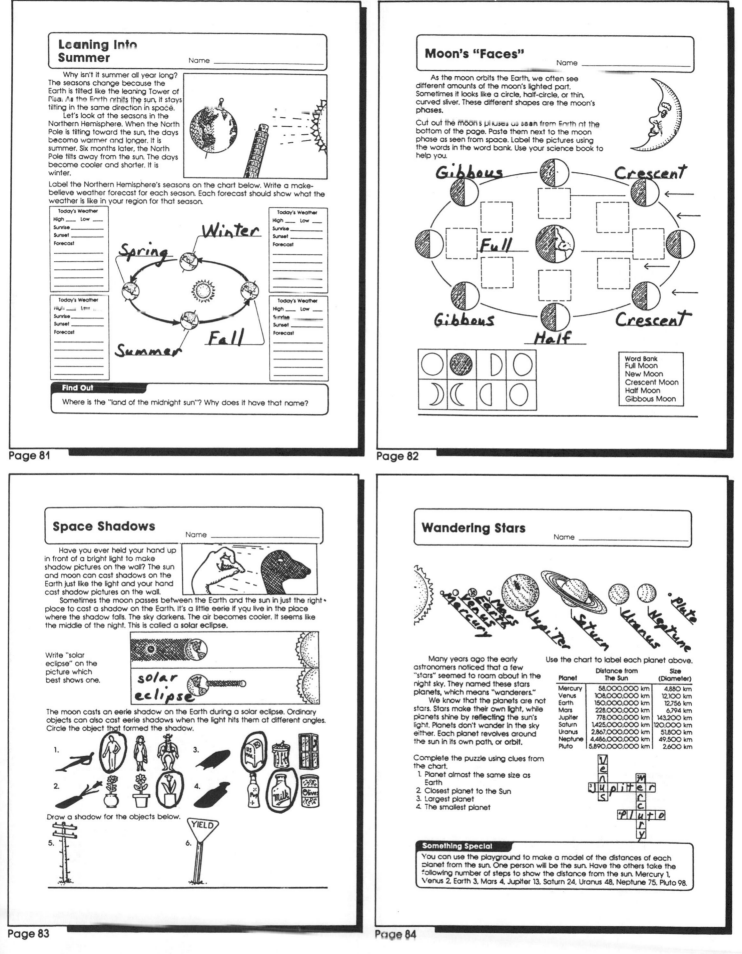

©1992 Instructional Fair, Inc.   123   IF8758 Science Enrichment

Answer Key

Planet Match

Name _____

Game Card

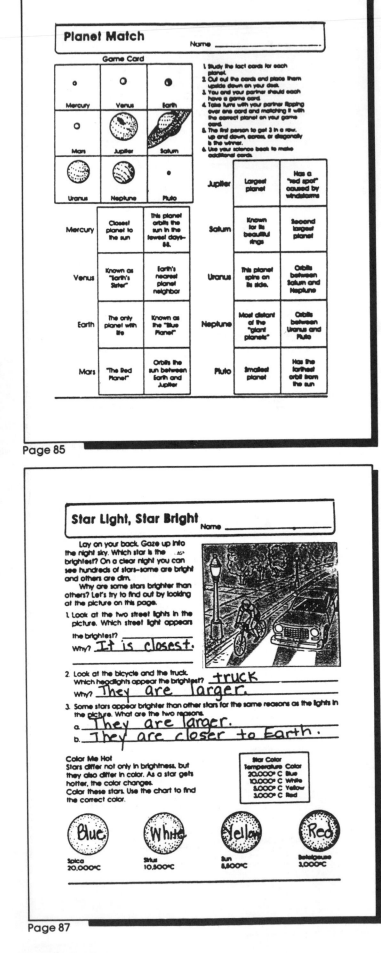

	Mercury	Venus	Earth
	Mars	Jupiter	Saturn
	Uranus	Neptune	Pluto

1. Study the fact cards for each planet.
2. Cut out the cards and place them upside down on your desk.
3. You and your partner should each have a game card.
4. Take turns with your partner flipping over one card and matching it with the correct planet on your game card.
5. The first person to get 3 in a row, up and down, across, or diagonally is the winner.
6. Use your science book to make additional cards.

Mercury	Closest planet to the sun	This planet orbits the sun in the fewest days—88.
Venus	Known as "Earth's Sister"	Earth's nearest planet neighbor
Earth	The only planet with life	Known as the "Blue Planet"
Mars	"The Red Planet"	Orbits the sun between Earth and Jupiter

Jupiter	Largest planet	Has a "red spot" caused by windstorms
Saturn	Known for its beautiful rings	Second largest planet
Uranus	This planet spins on its side.	Orbits between Saturn and Neptune
Neptune	Most distant of the "giant planets"	Orbits between Uranus and Pluto
Pluto	Smallest planet	Has the farthest orbit from the sun

Page 85

Space Snowballs

Name _____

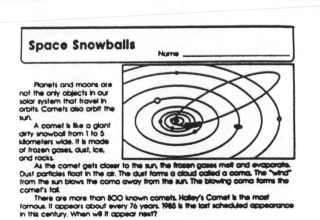

Planets and moons are not the only objects in our solar system that travel in orbits. Comets also orbit the sun.

A comet is like a giant dirty snowball from 1 to 5 kilometers wide. It is made of frozen gases, dust, ice, and rocks.

As the comet gets closer to the sun, the frozen gases melt and evaporate. Dust particles float in the air. The dust forms a cloud called a coma. The "wind" from the sun blows the coma away from the sun. The blowing coma forms the comet's tail.

There are more than 800 known comets. Halley's Comet is the most famous. It appears about every 76 years. 1985 is the last scheduled appearance in this century. When will it appear next?

Find the words from the word bank in the wordsearch. When you are finished, write down the letters that are not circled. Start at the top of the puzzle and go from left to right.

Word Bank

dust	orbit
Halley	tail
coma	ice
snowball	sky
dust	shining
solar system	melt

PLANETS HAVE ORBITS LIKE CIRCLES COMETS HAVE ORBITS SHAPED LIKE A FOOTBALL

Page 86

Star Light, Star Bright

Name _____

Lay on your back. Gaze up into the night sky. Which star is the brightest? On a clear night you can see hundreds of stars–some are bright and others are dim.

Why are some stars brighter than others? Let's try to find out by looking at the picture on this page.

1. Look at the two street lights in the picture. Which street light appears the brightest?
   Why? **It is closest.**

2. Look at the bicycle and the truck. Which headlights appear the brightest? **truck**
   Why? **They are larger.**

3. Some stars appear brighter than other stars for the same reasons as the lights in the picture. What are the two reasons.
   a. **They are larger.**
   b. **They are closer to Earth.**

Color Me Hot

Stars differ not only in brightness, but they also differ in color. As a star gets hotter, the color changes.
Color these stars. Use the chart to find the correct color.

Star Color	
Temperature	Color
20,000° C	Blue
10,000° C	White
5,000° C	Yellow
3,000° C	Red

Blue	White	Yellow	Red
Spica 20,000°C	Sirius 10,500°C	Sun 5,500°C	Betelgeuse 3,000°C

Page 87

Pictures in the Sky

Name _____

On a clear night, you can see hundreds of stars. You can probably see the Big Dipper or the Little Dipper. Try to make other pictures among the stars. Can you see animals or people?

Long ago, people spent hours gazing at the stars. They named groups of stars that formed pictures. We call these pictures constellations.

Color and cut out the constellations on this page. Make a mobile as pictured. Use your science book or other books to make pictures of other constellations for your mobile.

Cover a hanger with black paper and punch in holes to show some of your favorite constellations.

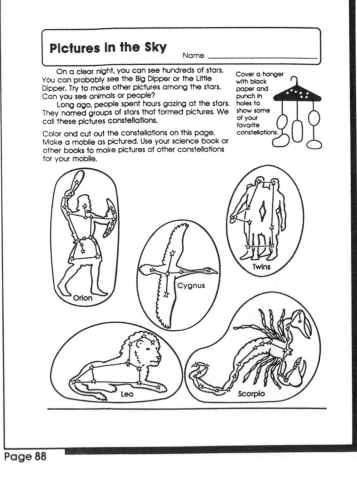

Orion — Cygnus — Twins — Leo — Scorpio

Page 88

©1992 Instructional Fair, Inc.

IF8758 Science Enrichment

Answer Key

Star Gazer (cover)

Name _____

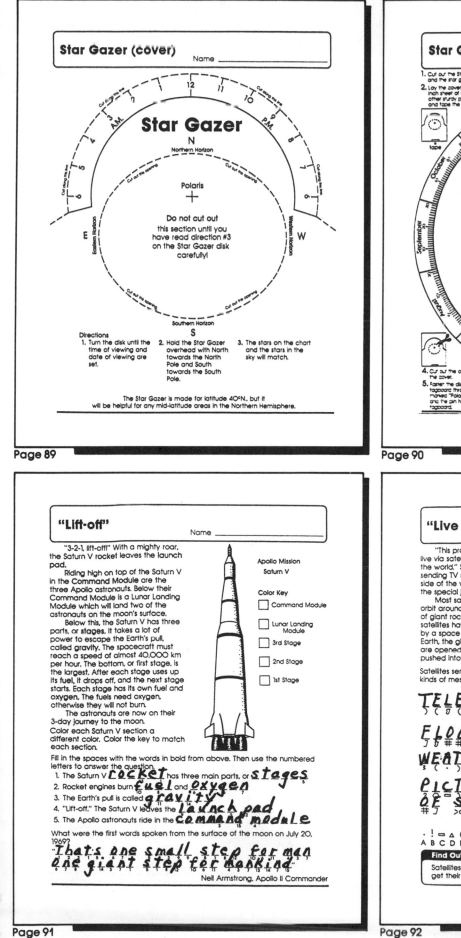

Star Gazer

N
Northern Horizon

Polaris
+

Do not cut out
this section until you
have read direction #3
on the Star Gazer disk
carefully!

E   W
Eastern Horizon   Western Horizon

S
Southern Horizon

Directions
1. Turn the disk until the time of viewing and date of viewing are set.
2. Hold the Star Gazer overhead with North towards the North Pole and South towards the South Pole.
3. The stars on the chart and the stars in the sky will match.

The Star Gazer is made for latitude 40°N., but it will be helpful for any mid-latitude areas in the Northern Hemisphere.

Star Gazer (disk)

Name _____

1. Cut out the Star Gazer disk and the star gazer cover.
2. Lay the cover on an 8 x 11 inch sheet of tagboard (or other sturdy paper). Line up and tape the bottom edge.
3. Make a pin hole through the cover and tagboard at the point marked "Polaris."

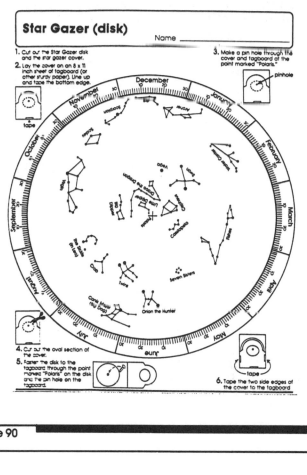

4. Cut out the oval section of the cover.
5. Fasten the disk to the tagboard through the point marked "Polaris" on the disk and the pin hole on the tagboard.
6. Tape the two side edges of the cover to the tagboard.

"Lift-off"

Name _____

"3-2-1, lift-off" With a mighty roar, the Saturn V rocket leaves the launch pad.

Riding high on top of the Saturn V in the Command Module are the three Apollo astronauts. Below their Command Module is a Lunar Landing Module which will land two of the astronauts on the moon's surface.

Below this, the Saturn V has three parts, or **stages**. It takes a lot of power to escape the Earth's pull, called **gravity**. The spacecraft must reach a speed of almost 40,000 km per hour. The bottom, or first stage, is the largest. After each stage uses up its fuel, it drops off, and the next stage starts. Each stage has its own fuel and oxygen. The fuels need oxygen, otherwise they will not burn.

The astronauts are now on their 3-day journey to the moon.
Color each Saturn V section a different color. Color the key to match each section.

Apollo Mission
Saturn V

Color Key
☐ Command Module
☐ Lunar Landing Module
☐ 3rd Stage
☐ 2nd Stage
☐ 1st Stage

Fill in the spaces with the words in bold from above. Then use the numbered letters to answer the question.
1. The Saturn V _rocket_ has three main parts, or _stages_.
2. Rocket engines burn _fuel_ and _oxygen_.
3. The Earth's pull is called _gravity_.
4. "Lift-off." The Saturn V leaves the _launch pad_.
5. The Apollo astronauts ride in the _command module_.

What were the first words spoken from the surface of the moon on July 20, 1969?
"That's one small step for man one giant step for mankind."

Neil Armstrong, Apollo II Commander

"Live Via Satellite"

Name _____

"This program is brought to you live via satellite from halfway around the world." Satellites are very helpful in sending TV messages from the other side of the world. But this is only one of the special jobs that satellites can do.

Most satellites are placed into orbit around the Earth by riding on top of giant rockets. Only recently some satellites have been carried into orbit by a space shuttle. While orbiting the Earth, the giant doors of the shuttle are opened, and the satellite is pushed into orbit.

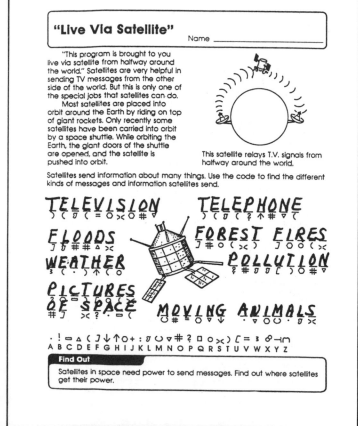

This satellite relays T.V. signals from halfway around the world.

Satellites send information about many things. Use the code to find the different kinds of messages and information satellites send.

TELEVISION   TELEPHONE
FLOODS   FOREST FIRES
WEATHER   POLLUTION
PICTURES   MOVING ANIMALS
OF SPACE

ABCDEFGHIJKLMNOPQRSTUVWXYZ

Find Out
Satellites in space need power to send messages. Find out where satellites get their power.

©1992 Instructional Fair, Inc.   125   IF8758 Science Enrichment

Answer Key

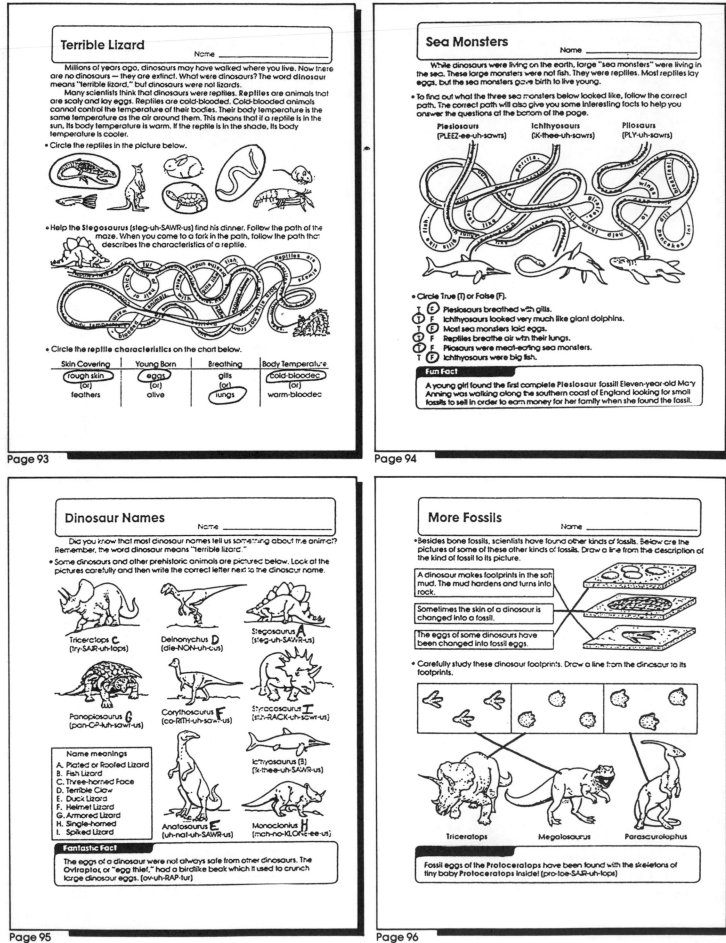

Terrible Lizard

Name _____

Millions of years ago, dinosaurs may have walked where you live. Now there are no dinosaurs — they are extinct. What were dinosaurs? The word dinosaur means "terrible lizard," but dinosaurs were not lizards.

Many scientists think that dinosaurs were reptiles. Reptiles are animals that are scaly and lay eggs. Reptiles are cold-blooded. Cold-blooded animals cannot control the temperature of their bodies. Their body temperature is the same temperature as the air around them. This means that if a reptile is in the sun, its body temperature is warm. If the reptile is in the shade, its body temperature is cooler.

• Circle the reptiles in the picture below.

• Help the Stegosaurus (steg-uh-SAWR-us) find his dinner. Follow the path of the maze. When you come to a fork in the path, follow the path that describes the characteristics of a reptile.

• Circle the reptile characteristics on the chart below.

Skin Covering	Young Born	Breathing	Body Temperature
(rough skin) (or) feathers	(eggs) (or) alive	gills (or) (lungs)	(cold-blooded) (or) warm-blooded

Page 93

Sea Monsters

Name _____

While dinosaurs were living on the earth, large "sea monsters" were living in the sea. These large monsters were not fish. They were reptiles. Most reptiles lay eggs, but the sea monsters gave birth to live young.

• To find out what the three sea monsters below looked like, follow the correct path. The correct path will also give you some interesting facts to help you answer the questions at the bottom of the page.

Plesiosaurs (PLEEZ-ee-uh-sawrs) Ichthyosaurs (ik-thee-uh-sawrs) Pliosaurs (PLY-uh-sawrs)

• Circle True (T) or False (F).

T (F) Plesiosaurs breathed with gills.
(T) F Ichthyosaurs looked very much like giant dolphins.
(T) F Most sea monsters laid eggs.
(T) F Reptiles breathe air with their lungs.
(T) F Pliosaurs were meat-eating sea monsters.
T (F) Ichthyosaurs were big fish.

Fun Fact
A young girl found the first complete Plesiosaur fossil! Eleven-year-old Mary Anning was walking along the southern coast of England looking for small fossils to sell in order to earn money for her family when she found the fossil.

Page 94

Dinosaur Names

Name _____

Did you know that most dinosaur names tell us something about the animal? Remember, the word dinosaur means "terrible lizard."

• Some dinosaurs and other prehistoric animals are pictured below. Look at the pictures carefully and then write the correct letter next to the dinosaur name.

Triceratops **C** (try-SAIR-uh-tops)
Deinonychus **D** (die-NON-uh-cus)
Stegosaurus **A** (steg-uh-SAWR-us)
Panoplosaurus **G** (pan-OP-luh-sawr-us)
Corythosaurus **F** (co-RITH-uh-sawr-us)
Styracosaurus **I** (sti-RACK-uh-sawr-us)
Anatosaurus **E** (uh-nat-uh-SAWR-us)
Ichthyosaurus (B) (ik-thee-uh-SAWR-us)
Monoclonius **H** (mon-no-KLONE-ee-us)

Name meanings
A. Plated or Roofed Lizard
B. Fish Lizard
C. Three-horned Face
D. Terrible Claw
E. Duck Lizard
F. Helmet Lizard
G. Armored Lizard
H. Single-horned
I. Spiked Lizard

Fantastic Fact
The eggs of a dinosaur were not always safe from other dinosaurs. The Oviraptor, or "egg thief," had a birdlike beak which it used to crunch large dinosaur eggs. (ov-uh-RAP-tur)

Page 95

More Fossils

Name _____

• Besides bone fossils, scientists have found other kinds of fossils. Below are the pictures of some of these other kinds of fossils. Draw a line from the description of the kind of fossil to its picture.

A dinosaur makes footprints in the soft mud. The mud hardens and turns into rock.

Sometimes the skin of a dinosaur is changed into a fossil.

The eggs of some dinosaurs have been changed into fossil eggs.

• Carefully study these dinosaur footprints. Draw a line from the dinosaur to its footprints.

Triceratops   Megalosaurus   Parasaurolophus

Fossil eggs of the Protoceratops have been found with the skeletons of tiny baby Protoceratops inside! (pro-toe-SAIR-uh-tops)

Page 96

©1992 Instructional Fair, Inc.

IF8758 Science Enrichment

Answer Key

Nippers, Rippers, and Grinders

Name _____

1. [skull image] 2. [skull image] 3. [skull image]

Scientists tell us that some of the dinosaurs were meat-eaters and others were plant-eaters. But how do the scientists know? By looking at the teeth of certain dinosaur fossils, scientists can tell what those dinosaurs ate. Meat-eaters had sharp, saw-edged teeth (figure 1), for cutting and ripping flesh. Plant-eating dinosaurs had either peg-like teeth (figure 2), for nipping plants, or flat grinding teeth (figure 3), to munch tough twigs or leaves.

1. Match the dinosaur to its teeth by writing its name in the space provided.
2. Circle either "M" for meat-eater or "P" for plant-eater.

Meat-eater or Plant-eater

Tyrannosaurus (tie-ran-o-SAWR-us) — Hypsilophodon — (M) P

Parasaurolophus (par-uh-sawr-uh-LOW-fus) — Monoclonius — M (P)

Monoclonius (mah-no-KLONE-ee-us) — Tyrannosaurus — (M) P

Hypsilophodon (HIP-sil-ahf-oh-don) — Parasaurolophus — M (P)

Triceratops (try-SAIR-uh-tops) — Triceratops — M (P)

The Tyrannosaurus, whose name means "king of the tyrant lizards," was the largest meat-eater. It weighed over 8 tons and was over 15 meters long. Its teeth were over 15 cm long and had edges like a steak knife.

Page 97

Dinosaur Framework

Name _____

Fossil bones are the only clues we have to tell us what the dinosaurs were like. Small, fast dinosaurs had very lightweight bones that were sometimes hollow. Big, heavy dinosaurs had thick bones to help support all their weight.

Dinosaurs were vertebrates. A vertebrate is an animal that has a backbone. A backbone is made of many smaller bones, called vertebrae. The vertebrae are connected to each other. Humans and all other mammals, reptiles, birds, fish, and amphibians that live today are vertebrates.

• Match the dinosaurs pictured below with the skeletons by putting the correct number next to each skeleton. Then with a crayon or marker, color the backbone of each dinosaur skeleton.

1. Plateosaurus 2. Brachiosaurus 3. Triceratops

4. Lesothosaurus 5. Tyrannosaurus 6. Spinosaurus

1 ___ 3 ___ 4 ___

6 ___ 2 ___ 5 ___

Page 98

Lumps, Bumps, and Scars

Name _____

It's exciting when a paleontologist (a scientist who studies fossils) finds a dinosaur fossil. The fossil might be from a dinosaur no one has ever discovered before.

It might take years for paleontologists to put together most of a dinosaur's bones. The lumps, bumps, and scars on the bones give them clues as to what the dinosaur might have looked like. These marks on the bones show where muscles were attached. By looking at the whole skeleton and the lumps, bumps, and scars on each bone, paleontologists can carefully guess the shape of the dinosaur's body.

• The two skeletons below are make-believe dinosaurs that nobody has ever found. Study the skeletons. Then use colored pencils, crayons, or markers to draw right over the skeleton, to show what these dinosaurs might have looked like. Name your dinosaurs.

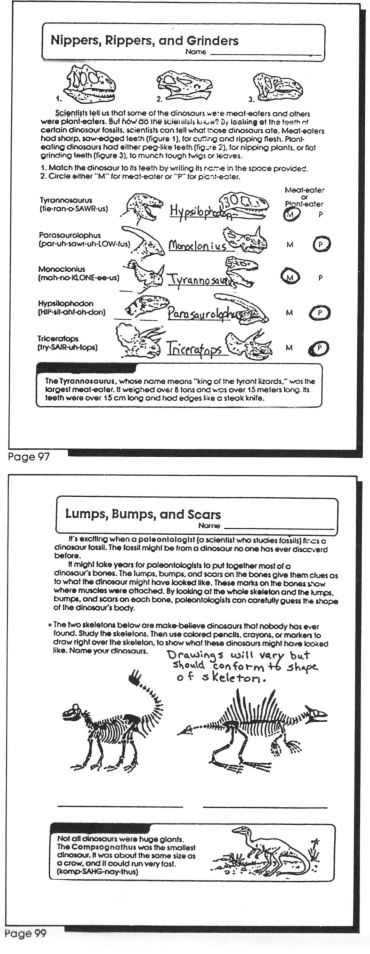

Drawings will vary but should conform to shape of skeleton.

_____   _____

Not all dinosaurs were huge giants. The Compsognathus was the smallest dinosaur. It was about the same size as a crow, and it could run very fast. (komp-SAHG-nay-thus)

Page 99

Dinosaur Defense

Name _____

How did the plant-eating dinosaurs protect themselves from the attacks of the fierce meat-eating dinosaurs? One way was to travel in groups. But they also had other ways to defend themselves. For example, some had horns and some could run very fast.

• Look at the plant-eating dinosaurs below. Find the features of their bodies that gave them protection from their enemies. Explain in the space provided.

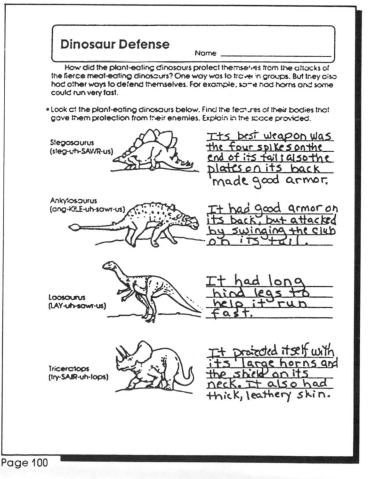

Stegosaurus (steg-uh-SAWR-us) — Its best weapon was the four spikes on the end of its tail; also the plates on its back made good armor.

Ankylosaurus (ang-KILE-uh-sawr-us) — It had good armor on its back, but attacked by swinging the club on its tail.

Laosaurus (LAY-uh-sawr-us) — It had long hind legs to help it run fast.

Triceratops (try-SAIR-uh-tops) — It protected itself with its large horns and the shield on its neck. It also had thick, leathery skin.

Page 100

Answer Key

Answer Key

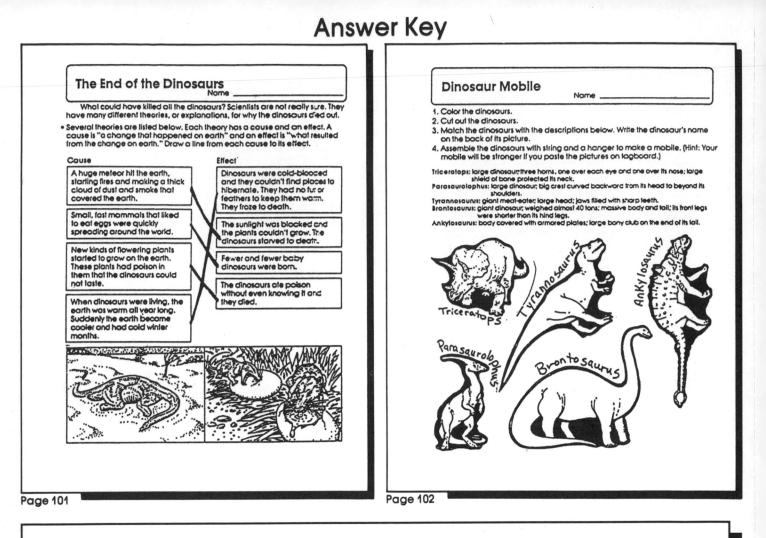

Page 101

Page 102

About the book . . .

This book will enhance your science program with entertaining, interesting and informative activities covering such diverse topics as plants, animals, astronomy, the human body, magnets and electricity, simple machines, plus more.

About the author . . .

Daryl Vriesenga holds a Master's Degree from Michigan State University in Science Education. He has taught at the elementary level for over eighteen years. He is the author of several science books for the elementary classroom, including **Science Fair Projects**, **Science Activities**, **Earth Science** and **The Human Body**, among others.

Credits . . .

Author: Daryl Vriesenga
Editor: Jackie Servis and Rhonda DeWaard
Artists: Sandra W. Ludwig, Dan Cool and Kurt Kemperman
Production: Pat Geasler and Mike Denhof
Cover Photo: Dan Van Duinen